I0161548

THE MENTAL GAME
OF SPEAKING

Building Composure,
Confidence and Credibility

Bill Cole MS MA

ABP

Copyright © 2017 William B. Cole

All rights reserved. Published in the U.S.A.

No part of this publication may be reproduced or transmitted in any form or by any means electronic or mechanical, including photocopying, recording or any information storage or retrieval system now known or to be invented, without permission from the publisher in writing, except by a reviewer who wishes to quote brief passages in connection with a review for inclusion in a magazine, newspaper, broadcast or website. Scanning and transmission of this book via the Internet, an intranet, or any other means without the permission of the publisher is illegal and punishable by law.

Special discounts on bulk quantities of Albert-Brownson Publishing books are available to corporations, professional associations, governmental entities and other organizations to use as sales promotions, premiums and training resources. Private imprints may also be arranged. For details, contact Albert-Brownson Publishing, 19925 Stevens Creek Blvd., Suite 100, Cupertino, CA 95014-2358, 408-725-7191.

International rights and foreign translations available only through negotiation with Albert-Brownson Publishing.

Library of Congress Cataloging In Publication Data

Cole, William B. The Mental Game Of Speaking: Building Composure, Confidence and Credibility

1. Reference 2. Communication 3. Business I. Title
ISBN: 978-1-931825-16-0: $19.95

TABLE OF CONTENTS

ASSESSING YOURSELF IN SPEAKING

WRITING PRESENTATIONS

PRACTICING PRESENTATIONS

AUDIENCE CALIBRATION

GETTING READY TO SPEAK

HANDLING STAGE FRIGHT

AVOID THESE SPEAKING ERRORS

BUILDING CONFIDENCE IN SPEAKING

WRITING AND USING HUMOR

QUESTION AND ANSWER SESSIONS

SPEAKING TO SPECIAL AUDIENCES

INFLUENCING SKILLS IN SPEAKING

CHECKLISTS & FORMS FOR SPEAKERS

Disclaimer

This book was written to provide information on public speaking, including speech analysis, speech writing, platform skills, stage fright, the psychology of speaking, how to practice, audience analysis, building confidence, writing and delivering speech humor, influencing skills, question-answer sessions, specialized speaking situations, and speaker forms and checklists.

The author and publisher are not engaged in rendering legal, accounting, psychological, career, counseling or other professional advice or services. If assistance of this type is sought, the services of the appropriate, competent professional should be consulted.

This publication does not contain all the available information about public speaking available to potential or current speakers. It instead attempts to supplement, support and add to existing texts and other information sources. The reader is encouraged to consult all pertinent available material, in all published forms, and adapt and customize the material to your specific speaking needs.

Public speaking is not a get-rich-quick business. This book does not purport or suggest that the public speaking business is easy to enter, easy to make money in, nor easy to stay in. Public speaking is a challenging industry, one that has risks, as any other business has. Anyone attempting to enter this field should expect to invest considerable time, money and effort to reach a level of success. Many individuals have transitioned to public speaking and have made solid, profitable careers that have lasted for years.

The author and publisher have made every effort to make this text as accurate and complete as possible. There may be, however, mistakes, both typographical and in content. Accordingly, this book should be used

1

only as a general guide and not as the ultimate authoritative source on the speaking industry. This publication contains information on the speaking business that is current only up to the printing date.

The purpose of this text is to educate and to entertain. The author and the publisher, Albert-Brownson Publishing, shall have neither liability nor responsibility to any person or entity with respect to any loss or damage caused or alleged to have been caused, directly or indirectly, by the information contained in this book.

If you do wish to be bound by the above, you may return this book to the publisher for a full refund.

Acknowledgements

I would like to thank those people who helped us in my speaking careers, either directly, or indirectly. I would like to specifically thank Craig Harrison, who encouraged me to run for election to the Board of Directors of the National Speakers Association, where I met an amazing collection of high-achieving individuals. I was very grateful to be a part of that Board and to have found a number of new speaking colleagues and friends there. Special thanks to Patricia Fripp, CSP, CPAE for her help during those years.

I would also like to thank Ken Braly and Robyn Holt for asking me to be part of their mastermind group for professional speakers, where I first met Michael Lee. That relationship with Michael started as one of mentoring and evolved into a co-authoring partnership culminating in this book.

I am forever grateful to my wonderful wife, Anli Lao Cole.

I owe a special thanks to my clients who teach me as I teach them.

Bill Cole, MS, MA

3

Dedication

The Mental Game Of Speaking is dedicated to my many clients over these years with whom I have been so privileged to serve.

What Is Not In This Book

The Mental Game of Speaking covers a wide variety of topics, issues, skills and content in public speaking. As the title implies, it has a specialized focus on the psychological aspects of presenting. As a peak performance coach of many years, that has been my specialty, and when speakers come to me for coaching, we cover that area in depth.

This book covers the essentials of what you need to know to be an excellent public speaker. We take a look at speech analysis, speech writing, platform skills, overcoming stage fright, the psychology of speaking, how to practice, audience analysis, building confidence, writing and delivering speech humor, influencing skills, question-answer sessions, specialized speaking situations, speaker forms and checklists and much more.

This book does not cover professional speaking career strategies, business skills, topic development, product development, fee setting, or knowledge of how the professional speaking world works. If you are interested in learning about those advanced professional topics and skills, I suggest you see my book on professional speaking, Free To Fee: How To Move Into The World Of Professional Speaking.

In my next book I may cover some of these topics:

1. The executive who speaks.

2. Speaking for association and business audiences.

3. Practicing a speech.

4. Writing articles for ezines, newsletters, magazines and newspapers.

5

5. Getting media attention.

6. Working with speaker bureaus.

7. Using Toastmasters as a launching pad.

8. Setting up a speaker website and blog.

9. Doing teleseminars and webinars.

10. How to create a demo video.

11. How to be a panelist and master of ceremonies (MC).

12. Print vs. digital marketing materials.

13. Back-of-room sales.

14. Showmanship and theatrics.

15. Acting and improv techniques.

16. Choreography and staging.

17. How to get income from no-fee engagements.

18. How to get a corporate sponsor.

19. Creative negotiating tactics for compensation.

20. Using barter and trade-outs.

21. How to speak on cruise ships.

22. Using high tech in presentations.

23. Using props in presentations.

24. Technical considerations when speaking.

25. Hiring a virtual assistant.

26. Hiring and using salespeople.

27. Doing seminars vs. workshops.

28. Setting up your business structure.

29. E-commerce shopping carts and accepting credit cards and PayPal.

30. Copyright and legal issues in speaking.

31. Public relations and promotions.

32. How to get testimonials.

33. Travel issues.

34. Speaking internationally.

35. How to set up a mastermind group.

36. Traditional book publishing vs. self-publishing.

37. Creating and using ezines, newsletters and mailing lists.

38. Appearing on TV, radio and podcasts.

What additional topics would you like to see me cover? Drop me a line and let me know.

How To Use This Book

I wrote this book so you can use it as your personal guide to the world of public speaking. How will you be using this book? Are you mainly speaking as part of your job? Do you speak at conferences, meetings and retreats? Maybe you're in toastmasters and wish to advance your knowledge and skills in this field. You may be a professional speaker and are seeking deeper levels of content so you can really wow your audiences and advance in the business.

Whatever your reasons for reading this book, welcome! I'm glad to have you on this journey.

I love speaking and I also love to study it and teach others the skills and strategies of public speaking.

This book does not need to be read in a linear manner from start to finish. Feel free to jump around and explore areas that you need right now.

The appendices contain specialized content that take you on a deeper dive into areas that master speakers need to know and master.

Some of the documents in the appendix are interactive checklists you can use for your speaking engagements.

There is a glossary of terms used in public speaking that are very handy to know. You'll use these all the time. Many people like to start here and get a sense of what is to come in the various chapters.

Introduction

This book is dedicated to helping you learn more about the skills and knowledge needed for excellence in public speaking, and in helping you become a more polished, confident speaker.

First, let me ask you some key questions about your speaking. You may want to use these as an assessment for how you could approach reading this book.

On what topics do you speak? In what type of speaking situations do you find yourself? How often do you speak? What types of audiences do you encounter? Do you speak in person, or virtually? How large are your audiences? How well can you build rapport and connection with your audiences? Do you know how to calibrate your audiences in real time? Do you know how to properly practice your speeches? Are you effective at handling the Q-A sessions in your programs? How good are you at writing your content for a speech? Do you know how to organize the elements of a good speech? Do you know how to memorize a speech? How convincing are you with audiences? Do they see you as having credibility? Can you sell yourself and your ideas? Do you use your sense of humor when you speak? Do you get paid to speak? How many years have you been speaking? Where do you want to go in your career in speaking? What sorts of obstacles have you been facing in your speaking? How well do you handle nerves? How confident are you? Do you have a plan to improve your speaking?

Those are the types of questions I ask my clients the first time I meet them. That helps us both know where they are currently and where they want to go.

In what different ways do you speak now? Here are the types of people I regularly coach:

- Executives speaking at meetings, retreats and industry events.

- Engineers moving into a sales or manager position.

- Academics, researchers and educators speaking at conferences.

- Physicians speaking as a media spokesperson.

- Speakers doing web casts and podcasts.

- Content experts giving industry speeches.

- Authors on TV and radio book tours.

- Politicians doing TV, radio, speeches and debates.

- Speakers, authors or actors shooting commercials and infomercials.

- Trainers moving into keynoting.

- Toastmasters who want to improve their speaking impact and maybe even move into paid professional speaking.

- Professional speakers wanting to move up a level.

- Business owners wanting to use speaking as a marketing vehicle.

- Business owners pitching a concept or business plan to investors.

- Salespeople giving team or individual presentations.

Whatever your speaking venue, audience and goals, if you're reading this book, there is content here that can help you improve and reach more of your potential.

My Coaching For Speakers

I coach people on all aspects of speaking, but early on in my career I started out by helping people overcome stage fright. That is still one of my specialized focus areas. I began my work in the field of sport psychology way back in the 1970's as a college undergraduate. The field was young and I was excited to learn that those tenets could be applied to a wide variety of areas. I still have a strong emphasis on sport psychology in my businesses, and I've expanded this work to many allied areas. I coach people using my mental game theme. I help people improve their ability to reduce stress and pressure, and convert it into positive excitement and peak performance. In addition to helping people through my presentation coaching, I do sales coaching, interview coaching and executive coaching. All of these require excellent presentation skills to be at your best.

What's In This Book

The Mental Game of speaking has over 50 chapters in 13 major sections. Here you will learn about the skills and knowledge top speakers possess, including strategies for writing speeches, practicing speeches, analyzing audiences, mentally preparing to speak and to overcome stage fright, how to become confident as a speaker, the use of humor, dealing with question and answer periods, and how to become a persuasive presenter. There are many unique one-of-a-kind checklists on virtually every aspect of speaking you'd like to know.

Here are the 13 major sections.

1. Assessing Yourself

2. Writing Presentations

3. Practicing Presentations

4. Audience Calibration

In reading this book you have access to hundreds of tips, tools and strategies that can help you dramatically improve your speaking. You can immediately apply these methods to any type of speaking you do.

How This Book Is Different

This book's special focus is on the psychology of speaking. My approach to the mental game of speaking helps people overcome stage fright, and inner obstacles and challenges that get in their way. Another unique strength of this book is its assessments. There are six of them. These help you become more aware of yourself as a speaker, and to make substantive changes, based on this feedback. There are two chapters on writing and practicing speeches, a chapter on how to pace your speeches, and six chapters on building confidence as a speaker. Few speaking books talk about body language. There is a chapter with a checklist of the 44 most common mistakes speakers make with their body language and a chapter on how to analyze, read and adjust to your audiences. Very few speaking books have content on the use of humor. Of course you can read entire books that cover the use of humor in speaking, but this book has four chapters on how to write, craft and use humor that can get you started.

There are three chapters on how to shine in the question-answer phase of your program. Most books on presentation skills don't have much emphasis on the special audiences we encounter. This book does. In it you'll find chapters on speaking to the boardroom, VIP's, and C-level executives. You can read a chapter on how to become an effective moderator and facilitator, and if you speak to the media, speak to foreign or international audiences, present on the web or the telephone, there are chapters for each of those. Probably the most vital skill for a speaker to possess is that of persuasion. There are two chapters on influencing skills. There are eight specialized checklists for speakers and a 218-word glossary of terms used in public speaking.

My Background In Speaking

I have been in professional speaking for many years. My current fee for a keynote program is $6,500 for 90 minutes. I have a training business in Silicon Valley, California and also have a coaching division in a variety of areas, all with the theme in peak performance, the mental game. I wrote this book as a presentation coach who speaks. I think that's important to actually be able to do what you teach others to do.

In 1974 I gave my first paid speech when I was asked to teach a college class in sport psychology for my professor, who was out of town. I was a college junior and received $25. I was paid, but I wasn't quite a professional speaker. I grew to love speaking and teaching, and as often as I could, I spoke at colleges and professional academic conferences in my field of sport psychology. I eventually taught college at three universities across the US for 15 years and thereby gained extensive experience standing in front of people delivering a message.

I owned a seminar business in New York State in the 1970's, doing "Zen Tennis" workshops, and again in the

1980's in Texas and California, doing them for tennis and golf, which I still do today. Through all these years my speaking topics focused on my brand, the mental game. I have been the mental game coach to athletes, coaches and parents in over 100 sports. My sports clients eventually asked me if I could teach these same principles for their businesses, such as peak performance in sales, and to overcome stage fright in public speaking. I said yes, and new divisions of my business were born. I started to see brand new applications of my mental game theme, and I began to widen it to customer service, stress, teambuilding, leadership and communication. I also developed a special niche as an interview coach from my extensive experiences from being interviewed by the media. All of these forms of coaching have elements of public speaking in them.

The effectiveness of my presentation coaching is based on my training, education and experience in peak performance, and also the knowledge and skills I have learned by undertaking extensive class work, seminars and workshops in this field, and in allied fields. I've been fortunate to rub elbows with many of the top professional speakers in the world, and took classes from many of them. I have attended specialized workshops and seminars on every aspect of the speaking business, including humor writing and performing, standup comedy, improv, platform skills, creating products, staging, showmanship, using technology in speaking and many more.

In the world of comedy, I was very fortunate to take classes from some major comedy gurus, such as touring comedian Kurtis Matthews, legendary humorist Larry Wilde and Gene Perret, Emmy Award winning writer on The Carol Burnett Show, and Head Writer for Bob Hope. I'm also a graduate of the San Francisco Comedy College.

16

How This Book Can Help You

This book gives you a broad overview of the essential skills required in public speaking, while also taking a deep dive into specialized psychological content that is not commonly discussed. The field of public speaking is far ranging, and no single book can do justice to all the knowledge required for excellence in speaking. The Mental Game of Speaking can be your launching pad for further exploration.

If you have never spoken in public, this book can give you a firm foundation. If you have been speaking, you can take your game to the next level. Whatever your purpose and your goals, I am glad to have you reading this book now, and I look forward to going with you on your public speaking journey. I know you will find the world of public speaking to be a highly rewarding one. It's a subject that you can continue learning about for years to come.

Bill Cole, MS, MA

Cupertino, California

" "

Thoughts About Speaking

The difference between a good speech and a great speech is the energy with which the audience comes to their feet at the end. Is it polite? Is it a chore? Are they standing up because their boss just stood up? No. You want it to come from their socks.

Rob Lowe as Sam Seaborn, The West Wing

If you want me to speak for an hour, I am ready today. If you want me to speak for just a few minutes, it will take me a few weeks to prepare.

Mark Twain

It is my ambition to say in ten sentences what other men say in whole books.

Nietzsche

ASSESSING YOURSELF
IN SPEAKING

Conquering Stage Fright

Take This Platform Performance Anxiety Assessment

You're about to walk out on stage and give a perform-ance in front of a large audience. You'd like to turn around and run, full speed, in the opposite direction.

Why?

You have a full-blown case of stage fright, that's why.

If you're reading this, there's almost no need to explain what stage fright is and what it does to you. You know already.

Stage fright:

1. Can kill your performance.

2. Always causes you great stress.

3. May ruin your career.

4. Might have repercussions for your entire life.

5. Might make you avoid performing ever again.

6. Stage Fright Has Many Names

What do you call stage fright? It's been referred to in many ways, and has many variations and degrees of severity. Here are some of the more common names:

Performance anxiety

1. Acting panic

2. Test anxiety

3. Interview panic

4. Choking

5. Nerves

6. Nervous apprehension

7. Speaking anxiety

8. Actor's nerves

9. Show and tell stress

10. Fear of performing

11. Shyness

12. Social inhibition

13. Social anxiety

The Facts About Stage Fright

It's reassuring and powerful to realize these essential truths about what scares you. The first step to getting this fear response under your control is to demystify it.

1. Stage fright is normal. If you're human, you're going to get it.

2. Stage fright hits everyone, even the most experienced performers, at every level.

3. Stage fright is listed as the number one fear in the world.

4. The greatest names in the history of the world admit they suffer from stage fright.

5. You will never completely conquer stage fright, yet you can manage it.

6.   The more mind tools you have to beat stage fright, the better you will perform.

7.   Top performers turn in wonderful performances all the time, even though they are suffering from stage fright during the actual performance.

8.   Beating stage fright is not about being perfect or about being fear-free. It's about adjusting and managing your anxiety and using it to fuel your performances.

What Causes Stage Fright?

People rarely get stage fright singing in the shower. There's no audience there and no consequences if you mess up. Add an audience and some importance to the situation and you have the potential for a nice case of stage fright.

So why does it happen?

1.   Your body's chemistry kicks in to get you ready to perform.

2.   You may inaccurately misinterpret those feelings that you are "nervous".

3.   You mistakenly believe nerves to be "bad".

4.   You then worry that this is proof that you are about to fail and embarrass yourself.

5.   You then worry about worrying.

6.   The negative cycle continues.

7.   You selectively choose further nervousness proof that you are panicking and about to fail.

8.   All these symptoms combine to ignite a full-blown attack of nerves.

Bingo. You have a bad case of stage fright.

The Symptoms Of Stage Fright

Here are 75 symptoms of stage fright that people I've coached have described to me. You may want to use this as a self-assessment and rate yourself to see specifically how stage fright affects you.

1.   Shaking legs

2.   Wobbly knees

3.   Racing thoughts

4.   Irrational thoughts

5.   Feeling nauseous

6.   Pounding heart

7.   Shortness of breath

8.   Sweaty palms

9.   Tingling sensations

10.   Headaches

11.   Racing heartbeat

12.   Heart beat may seem louder

13.   Poor motor control

14.   Trembling hands

15.   Can't catch breath

16.   Flashbacks

17.   Thinking something bad is going to happen

18.   Feeling you will die

19. General anxiety, with no anchor

20. Nausea

21. Constipation

22. Disconnection with self

23. Numbness in body

24. Muscle tension

25. Moodiness

26. Avoidance behaviors

27. Rushing

28. Freezing

29. Negative thinking

30. Fearful imagery

31. Nightmares

32. Eating too much

33. Inability to eat

34. Avoidance of people

35. Inability to control thoughts

36. Inability to control images

37. Breath very high in chest

38. Hyperventilation

39. Voice may crack

40. Difficulty concentrating

41. Sudden tiredness

42. Emotional flatness

43. Insomnia

44. Fear the anxiety will spiral out of control

45. Breathing difficulty

46. Dizziness

47. Memory loss

48. Sensory deprivation

49. Cold palms

50. Sweaty palms

51. Voice may constrict and pitch may increase

52. Dry throat

53. Negative thoughts

54. Stiff movements

55. Poor coordination

56. Stumbling and bumbling

57. Heavy legs

58. Frozen movements

59. Stiff neck and shoulder

60. Impaired vision and hearing

61. Impaired sense of timing

62. Self-consciousness

63. Butterflies/queasiness in stomach

64. Cold feet

65. Shaking voice

66. Obsessive thoughts

67. Poor balance

68. Distorted sense of elapsed time

69. Tunnel vision

70. Panic attack

71. Spinning sensations

72. Blushing

73. Sudden heat in body

74. Uncomfortable feelings

75. Feeling cold for no reason

Conquering Stage Fright

Let me give you an overview of how to minimize the destructive powers of stage fright. You want to create a mental training system that gives you powers of self-regulation under extreme stress. You should have these mental game skills:

1. Learn a relaxation system.

2. Master a self-discipline system.

3. Devise a pre-program psych-up system.

4. Learn how to adjust mentally in your performance.

5. Set your attitude so you place less pressure on yourself.

6. Discover approaches that will get you into the zone.

7. Develop an in-performance mistake-management system.

8. Learn how to stay positive under pressure.

9. Find ways to enjoy yourself when you perform.

10. Use performing as a way to discover yourself.

11. Devise ways to connect with your audience.

12. Learn to rise above stress control to inspire yourself.

13. Create the conditions to perform to your potential.

Finally, don't give up. The only people who fail to conquer stage fright are those who quit performing. Even the most severe cases of stage fright can be helped. If you knew the many famous people in the public eye on TV, radio, movies and the stage who have overcome the worst cases of stage fright imaginable, you would be shocked. They did, and so can you.

Hang in there. There is hope.

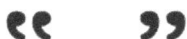

❝ ❞
Thoughts About Speaking

It's the space you put between the notes
that make the music.

Massimo Vignelli

So much is said with the electricity of the eyes,
the intensity of a whisper. Less is more.

Elizabeth Taylor

If it takes a lot of words to say what you have in mind,
give it more thought.

Dennis Roth

Common Fears And Concerns People Have About Presentations

As a long-time presentation coach, I hear many common fears and concerns from clients that get in the way of them performing well. Any of these concerns, if left unaddressed, can easily derail your performance, and hold you back from feeling confident, delivering your message effectively, and in managing the image to the audience that you desire.

Let's take a look at these various fears and worries people have about going into a presentation situation.

1. My mind might go blank.

2. It might be obvious that I'm afraid.

3. The audience might verbally attack me.

4. I could be embarrassed.

5. I could make a fatal mistake.

6. I may not know the answer to a question.

7. The audience may think my content is too minimal or thin.

8. The audience may think my material is weak.

9. The audience may think my material is disorganized.

10. I could get confused on questions from the audience.

11. I might lose my place.

12. I might make a mistake, and not know how to recover.

13. My voice might crack.

14. I don't know what good eye contact is.

15. I'm terrible at small talk and rapport prior to and after my program.

16. The audience might see that I am unprepared.

17. The audience may criticize me.

18. The audience may be very unfriendly.

19. The audience might ask crazy, nonsense or unintelligible questions.

20. I might fumble my papers or other materials.

21. I might stutter or stammer.

22. I have no idea how to handle an award presentation.

23. I don't know how to present someone.

24. I don't know what I should do differently in a keynote vs. a training session.

25. What do I do if the audience does not think my presentation is entertaining?

26. I'm confused about a speaking situation as compared to a teaching situation.

27. I'm scared to do TV or radio.

28. I have no clue how to speak to the press.

29. I've been asked to make an audio recording and I am clueless as to how to approach that.

30. I speak fine to a real audience, but I am lost when it comes to web or telephone presentations.

31. I set the room up haphazardly for my presentation, and I need help.

32. What do I do if my equipment malfunctions?

33. I'm terrible at creating and using PowerPoint and handouts.

34. I seem to have no talent for making my program experiential.

35. How do I create speech titles?

36. I'm not naturally funny. How do I inject some humor into my talks?

37. How do I create rapport with the audience?

38. What is advance work with the audience?

39. How do I make transitions in a talk?

40. I don't know how to practice my talk.

41. How do I write a speech?

42. How do I show passion in a talk?

43. What is WIFFM?

44. What is AIDA?

45. How do I vary my sentence structure and vocabulary?

46. How do I tell a great story?

47. Should I use props in my program?

48. I've heard of staging, but I don't know what that is.

49. How do I use my introduction to set up the talk?

50. I have a feeling I need help with my body language.

51. My energy tends to be flat when I speak.

52. Should I memorize my talk, or portions of it?

53. How can I use pauses for good effect?

54. How fast should I speak?

55. How can I avoid distracting and repeated mannerisms?

56. What is "writing the speech for the ear"?

57. How do I use a microphone?

58. Are there differences in speaking in small intimate settings as compared to large venues?

59. How do I create and use audience memory and organization devices?

60. How do I give a natural and spontaneous seeming delivery, even if I am well-rehearsed?

61. Should I walk and talk, or stand still?

62. Should I use the entire stage, the entire hall or stand behind the lectern?

63. What is a podium as compared to a lectern?

64. Should I read directly from notes or visuals?

34

65. How do I give less of a formal speech and make it more of an informal conversation?

66. How do I make a concluding statement that has impact?

67. How do I help the audience use what I have told them?

68. What is a speaker rating form and how do I use it?

69. Should I take questions as I go, or hold them until the end?

70. Why do I need to repeat questions to the entire audience?

71. How can I show the proper attention and respect to questioners?

72. How can I use questions as a vehicle to cover additional material?

73. What should I do if no one has any questions? That would be embarrassing.

74. How do I handle irrelevant or off-topic questions?

75. The audience may not like me. What do I do?

76. The audience might be argumentative or confrontational.

77. The audience may challenge my content.

78. I might have a panic attack.

79. My nervous laughter may be misinterpreted as being weak.

80. Maybe I won't be able to understand an audience member due to their accent.

81. I might get asked to stop the presentation or cut it short.

82. The audience might laugh at me.

83. The audience might be rude to me.

84. I might stumble, physically.

85. I may get tongue-tied.

86. I get very uncomfortable if there is a long silence.

87. I don't know how to show passion and interest.

88. There might be a disruption in the middle of the presentation.

89. The audience might use a word or term I don't know.

90. The audience might criticize my credibility.

91. I don't know what to do with my hands.

92. I might come across as too passive or boring.

93. How can I hide my lack of confidence?

94. I do well in practice, but I choke in real presentations.

95. How do I analyze the audience?

96. I have trouble remembering what I am going to say.

97. I speak in a monotone, so I sound boring.

98. My accent makes me hard to understand.

99. I tend to run my sentences together, making me hard to understand.

100. I don't know how to open the presentation.

101. I don't know how to close the presentation.

102. I talk way too fast, particularly when I'm nervous.

103. It feels like the presentation spins out of control and I can't get a handle on the clock.

104. I hate having to talk about myself.

105. How do I sell myself?

106. I am easily intimidated and shy with people I don't know.

107. Some of my answers are awful, and I dread being asked certain questions.

108. I might ramble on forever.

109. The audience might probe my answers.

110. The presentation format might be changed at the last minute.

111. I might suddenly have to go to the bathroom.

112. I might be asked to demonstrate something.

113. I may not get any applause.

114. I don't know the proper voice volume to use.

115. How do I know when the audience might be asking a trick question?

116. What do I do if the audience seems bored with me?

117. When I make a mistake I blame myself mercilessly and as a result, immediately make another

118. How do I stop using filler words like um, uh, and you know?

119. How do I get the audience's attention if they are wandering or distracted or just not paying me any attention?

120. What do I do if the audience starts asking about a topic I have no clue about?

121. How do I stall for time if I am stumped on a question?

122. What do I do if I begin a line of thought, realize I am on the wrong track, and want to change?

Now you know what issues bother you in speaking. Work toward discovering how to remove these obstacles so you can feel more secure and confident on the platform. Many of the solutions to these issues will be found in this book. For the other issues, I suggest you consult an experienced speaking coach who can assist you.

" " Thoughts About Speaking

You can speak well if your tongue
can deliver the message of your heart.

John Ford

If you wing it when speaking, you'll get wing it results.

Arvee Robinson

Take advantage of every opportunity to practice your
communication skills, so that when important occasions
arise, you will have the gift, the style, the sharpness,
the clarity, and the emotions to affect other people.

Jim Rohn

Presentation Analysis Chart

This is an evaluation checklist you can utilize both before and after your speaking program. It helps you organize every aspect of your program, including planning, writing, audience analysis, the purpose and theme of your talk, technical considerations, and much more. After your program you can use this to see how well you executed your plan.

Speaker Name _____

Program Title _____

Audience _____

Date/Location _____

The Purpose And Context Of Your Performance

Check as many as apply:

1. ____ Audience makes a decision.

2. ____ You make a suggestion or recommendation.

3. ____ You sell the audience something.

4. ____ You make an audience request.

5. ____ You have solutions.

6. ____ You present a problem.

7. ____ Marketing yourself.

8. ____ Entertainment.

9. ____ Award presentation or acceptance.

10. ____ Master of ceremonies.

11. ____ Commencement speech.

12. ____ Keynote speech.

13. ____ Breakout session.

14. ____ Training or teaching.

15. ____ Radio or television interview.

16. ____ Press Conference.

17. ____ Sales presentation.

18. ____ Teleconference.

19. ____ Web broadcast.

20. ____ Studio recording session.

21. ____ Infomercial.

22. ____ Debate.

23. ____ Interview for a job.

24. ____ Performance review.

Scoring. Mark a number for each item. 5 is excellent, 4 very good, 3 average, 2 fair and 1 poor.

Audience Analysis

1. ____ Noted time of day to account for attention problems?

2. ____ Noted knowledge level(s) of the audience.

3. ____ Matched level of formality expected.

4. ____ Matched dress code for the audience and speaker.

5. ____ Noted room layout and characteristics.

6. ____ Noted nearby rooms and space considerations for noise, etc.

7. ____ Noted biased audience members for or against your material.

8. ____ Noted how much audience know each other.

Considerations Regarding Time

1. ____ Equipment manipulation.

2. ____ People moving.

3. ____ Change of technology.

4. ____ Equipment breakdown.

5. ____ Distributing handouts.

6. ____ Questions and answers.

7. ____ Exercises.

8. ____ Breaks.

9. ____ Transitions.

Before You Get To The Program

1. ____ Selected appropriate speech title and sub-title.

2. ____ Sent AV and other needs to planner.

3. ____ Sent and gathered planner PP.

4. ____ Sent and gathered audience questionnaires.

5. ____ Analyzed audience.

6. ____ Assessed speech facilities.

7. ____ Integrated audience and planner material into talk.

8. ____ Integrated additional research material into talk.

9. ____ Practiced stories, humor, transitions, opening and closing.

10. ____ Performed dress rehearsal.

Developing The Speech

1. ____ Determined speech objectives.

2. ____ Defined scope of material.

3. ____ Matched material to time allotment.

4. ____ Drafted speech outline.

5. ____ Storyboarded the talk.

6. ____ Created flexible modules.

7. ____ Created production timelines.

Organization And Writing

1. ____ Each point supported your theme.

2. ____ Presented evidence on both sides of an issue.

3. ____ Presented historical perspective.

4. ____ Related your personal interest in the material.

5. ____ Utilized credible sources.

6. ___ Stated a thesis or point of the talk.

7. ___ The talk clearly demonstrated your audience research.

8. ___ Provided context for material.

9. ___ Continually reinforced the material's benefits for the audience.

10. ___ Varied your sentence structure and vocabulary.

Pre-Speech On-Site

1. ___ Schmooze factor.

2. ___ Image to audience.

3. ___ Arrived in advance for time cushion.

4. ___ Gathered stories, names, incidents to insert into talk.

5. ___ Interaction with AV and staff people.

6. ___ Room and stage set up.

7. ___ Organized assistants and staffers.

8. ___ Handouts, props, magic, costumes, etc.

9. ___ Equipment security.

Technical

1. ___ Decided on media.

2. ___ Created speaker notes.

3. ___ Created staging.

4. ___ Created audience handouts.

5. ____ Ordered required equipment.

6. ____ Test ran presentation.

Visual Aids

1. ____ Limited to one idea per slide or screen.

2. ____ Screen added to your text, and did not repeat it.

3. ____ Easily seen from a distance.

4. ____ Easily read fonts and point sizes.

5. ____ Colors were pleasing and easy to read.

6. ____ Good use of white space.

7. ____ Amount of text and graphics per screen were clean.

8. ____ Used persuasive slide titles.

9. ____ Visuals were not gratuitous or showy.

10. ____ Visuals were professional looking.

Your Introduction

1. ____ Started on time.

2. ____ Practiced introduction with intro person.

3. ____ Proper length.

4. ____ Intentional image as intro is read.

5. ____ Flowed into speaker opening.

6. ____ Created expectancy.

7. ____ Set the agenda, scope and theme.

8. ____ Grabbed the audience's attention quickly and firmly.

9. ____ Sold the importance and relevance of the topic to the audience.

10. ____ Built rapport and connection.

11. ____ Laid out the benefits of the talk to the audience.

12. ____ Confirmed your credibility for giving the talk.

13. ____ Told personal item connected to the theme and the audience.

Your Opening

1. ____ Accepted audience applause.

2. ____ Walk to platform.

3. ____ Body language.

4. ____ Energy.

5. ____ Looked at everyone before speaking.

6. ____ Warmth and smiles.

7. ____ Came out punching.

8. ____ Memorized opening.

9. ____ Opening had impact.

10. ____ Told audience reason for talk.

11. ____ Audience connection and rapport.

12. ____ Set proper tone.

13. ____ Set proper context.

14. ___ Humor.

Conversion Into Main Body Of Speech

1. ___ Connection of opening remarks to intro.

2. ___ Summarized what will happen in the talk.

3. ___ Made an agreement with the audience.

Middle Of Speech

1. ___ Made main points.

2. ___ Poise.

3. ___ Stories.

4. ___ Humor.

5. ___ Quotes.

6. ___ Facts.

7. ___ White space.

8. ___ Transitions.

9. ___ Pacing.

10. ___ Rapport.

11. ___ Housekeeping issues.

12. ___ Audience involvement exercises.

13. ___ Body language.

14. ___ Clothing or costumes.

15. ___ Facial expressions.

16. ___ Eye contact.

17. ____ Vocal variation.

18. ____ Vocal volume.

19. ____ Vocal tone.

20. ____ Use of language.

21. ____ Pronunciation.

22. ____ Understandability.

23. ____ Accent reduction sounded natural.

24. ____ Avoided distracting and repeated mannerisms.

25. ____ Wrote speech for the ear.

26. ____ Sufficient detail, but not too much.

27. ____ Used material from PPQ research.

28. ____ Thanked appropriate people.

29. ____ Interacted well with staff and AV people.

30. ____ Addressed current topics in days news.

31. ____ Addressed "what's on their mind".

32. ____ Avoided sensitive issues.

33. ____ Use of microphone.

34. ____ Use of media.

35. ____ Use of music and magic.

36. ____ Audience handouts.

37. ____ Props.

38. ____ Used money phrase(s).

39. ____ Continually addressed the WIFFM angle.

40. ____ Free of sexist, genderist, classist, ageist language.

41. ____ Matched formality level of audience.

42. ____ Used frequent summarization.

43. ____ Used audience memory and organization devices.

44. ____ Audience interaction...

45. ____ Natural and spontaneous seeming delivery (even if well-rehearsed).

46. ____ Diction was free of slang and jargon, unless used strategically.

47. ____ Use of "filler words and phrases" was limited (Um, you know, etc.).

48. ____ Used white space between thoughts.

49. ____ Avoided pauses mid-sentence.

50. ____ Used hand and body language to support content.

51. ____ Enthusiasm was evident to audience.

52. ____ Did not read directly from notes or visuals.

53. ____ Maintained eye contact with the audience.

54. ____ Had a conversation with the audience.

55. ____ Asked challenging and stimulating questions.

56. ____ Handled difficult audience members.

57. ____ Handled difficult situations.

58. ____ Use of entire stage.

59. ____ Moved into audience.

60. ____ Use of speaker notes.

End Of Speech

1. ____ Summarized major points.

2. ____ Q and A session.

3. ____ Handled objections.

4. ____ Restated your main points.

5. ____ Helped the audience use what you have told them.

6. ____ Made a concluding statement.

7. ____ Made a call to action.

8. ____ Speaker rating form handed out and collected.

9. ____ Reminded audience of their tasks after program.

Questions And Answers

1. ____ Allowed time for questions.

2. ____ Created proper atmosphere to encourage questions.

3. ____ Proper attention and respect shown to questioners.

4. ____ Stepped toward questioner.

5. ____ Appeared non-defensive and open to questions.

6. ____ Repeated questions to audience.

7. ____ Gave answers to entire audience.

8. ____ Avoided evaluating worth of question (That's a good one, etc.).

9. ____ Answered questions fully.

10. ____ Used questions as vehicle to cover additional material.

11. ____ Clarified poorly worded questions.

12. ____ Handled irrelevant or off-topic questions with tact.

13. ____ Promised to research questions that could not be fully answered.

14. ____ Prepared additional slides/screen to handle questions.

Your Closing

1. ____ Made one ending, not multiple.

2. ____ Smooth, not too abrupt.

3. ____ Ended on time.

4. ____ Made the ask.

5. ____ Memorable closing.

6. ____ Accepted audience's applause.

Post-Talk

1. ____ Stage exit.

2. ____ Schmooze factor.

3. ____ Product sales.

4. ____ Room and equipment tear-down.

5. ____ Had rapport with planner.

6. ____ Returned equipment and materials.

7. ____ Analyzed speaker rating sheets.

8. ____ Self-analysis of program.

Overall Summary

Rate the presentation 1-5 with 5 being excellent, 4 very good, 3 average, 2 fair and 1 poor. This presentation: _____.

1. What I really LIKED about this presentation:

2. What I wish I WOULD have done this time:

3. What I wish I would had NOT done this time:

4. What FEEDBACK did people give me?

5. What I would do DIFFERENTLY next time:

6. What I LEARNED from this presentation:

❝   ❞

Thoughts About Speaking

Oratory should raise your heart rate. Oratory should
blow the doors off the place.

Rob Lowe as Sam Seaborn, The West Wing TV show

Be who you are and say what you feel, because those
who mind don't matter, those who matter don't mind.

Dr. Seuss

Let he who would be moved to convince others be first
moved to convince himself.

T. Carlyle

WRITING
PRESENTATIONS

Ten Top Tips For Writing A Memorable Speech

When you sit in the audience enjoying a wonderful speech, the speaker's words seem to all make sense. They seem to be well-organized and easy to follow. One thought seems to fit with the next in a tight jig-saw puzzle kind of way. The speech is logical, interesting, convincing, entertaining and has a nice flow to it. You seem to be gently and effortlessly led along by the speaker's words. It's a small slice of heaven, isn't it?

What we see and hear as effortless speech-making actually comes from diligent, intelligent, sophisticated speech-writing. It comes from someone sitting down and crafting a thoughtful, smart, strategic set of concepts turned into practical tips, stories and action items. What the audience hears is music to their ears, almost literally.

Do you have a speech coming up soon? Need to write a talk that will grab your audience and make them sit on the edge of their seats? Take a moment to learn these ten essential elements of speech-writing and you may just give the speech of your life.

Ten Strategies For Crafting Excellent Speeches

1. **Prepare Early.** Begin gathering material for your speech right away. As you learn more about your topic, new ideas for writing and organizing it will automatically come to you.

2. **Be Audience-Centered.** Everything you write should be with the needs of the audience in mind. Aim all your efforts at helping the audience understand what you are saying.

3. **Start At The End First.** Write the conclusion of your talk right away. Decide what you want the audience to do or to think as a result of your speech. Then write the talk using that as a guide.

4. **Write For The Ear, Not The Eye.** Experienced writers know that every medium and project has its own language, cadence, style and structure. Don't write the speech to be read. You need to write your speech so when your audience hears it, they get it.

5. **Make Rough Drafts First And Polish Later.** Don't needlessly pressure yourself by trying to write the perfect speech at the outset. The best speeches come only after many, many re-writes.

6. **Put Your Own Spin On The Material.** You may block your creative juices if you think everything you say has to be original. Don't worry about being unique, just put your personal spin on it. The audience wants to hear your personal point of view.

7. **Make Only Three Main Points.** It is always tempting to tell as much as you can about a subject, but this will confuse and overwhelm your audience. Keep your major points to three and your audience will find it easier to follow your speech organization.

8. **Craft A Take-away Line.** When people can't make a speaker's session, they ask others who were there, "What did the speaker talk about?" What they say you said is your take-away line. You'd like people to walk out with that nugget. It's like creating street buzz for yourself.

9. **Decide The Least And Most Critical.** What is the very least the audience needs to know about your topic? What is the most critical? Leave out

material that would be "nice to know". You probably won't have time for it anyhow.

10. **Write Using The WIIFM principle.** WIIFM is when your audience responds to your material by asking themselves "What's In It For Me?" People are really only interested in material that affects them. After writing any piece of material, no matter how brilliant, apply the WIIFM principle and judge if your audience will care about it and use it.

Three Bonus Tips For Writing A Great Speech

1. **Write As If You Are Conversing With One Person.** How many times have you felt the speaker was talking directly only to you? This phenomenon is in part, an acting and speaking technique, but it also stems from how the speech is written. As you write, picture one person and what you want to say to them. Then write the speech.

2. **Decide What You Want Your Audience To Do Or Think Differently As A Result Of Your Speech.** There is really only one reason to give a speech. That's to have your audience either make a change in their thinking or their behavior. Otherwise, what's the point? Decide what you want for them and then write your speech around that.

3. **Use "Audience-Involvement" Devices.** To bring the audience into your talk and to make sure they are engaged, craft numerous interactive techniques. These can be questions, exercises, role plays, verbal quizzes and other ways that get them actively involved with your material.

So there you have it, ten quick tips for writing better and more memorable speeches. When you write your speeches, remember these and your audience will thank you by giving you their rapt attention.

" "

Thoughts About Speaking

Half the world is composed of people who have something to say and can't, and the other half who have nothing to say and keep on saying it.

Robert Frost

...and from the first moment that I ever walked on stage in front of a darkened auditorium with a couple of hundred people sitting there, I was never afraid, I was never fearful, I didn't suffer from stage fright, because I felt so safe on that stage. I wasn't Patrick Stewart, I wasn't in the environment that frightened me, I was pretending to be someone else, and I liked the other people I pretended to be. So I felt nothing but security for being on stage. And I think that's what drew me to this strange job of playing make-believe.

Patrick Stewart

Feel the fear of public speaking and do it anyway.

Arvee Robinson

Writing And Delivering
Very Brief Speeches

"Be Good, Be Brief, and Be Seated"

You've probably heard the well-known old joke about letter writing.

"This is a very long letter because I did not have time to write a short one."

It exactly applies to when you are giving a short talk.

In the speech game, if you don't take the time to craft a tight, focused presentation before you deliver a short talk, you will lose your audience. You may also lose your reputation.

For any length speech you have to craft the talk well, practice it well and deliver it well. This is true for ANY length presentation, but unfortunately, speakers often treat a brief talk as inconsequential. "This is only a five-minute talk, so I'll just wing it. No need to practice such a short speech" they think. This mind set can lead to disaster. Smart speakers know better. They treat ALL talks as important.

Let's take a look at the ten most critical features of crafting and delivering short speeches.

1.   The writing for shorter speeches has to better than for long ones. You have less time to get your critical message across.

2.   You must make sure the audience gets the central core theme of your message... and right away.

3.   You have no luxury of "warming up" your audience as you sometimes can do in a longer

talk or seminar. You must "make the first impression the best".

4. You have no time for wandering around or chaff. Go off on a tangent and in a flash your time will be up and you will be sitting down...with your audience wondering what in the world you just said.

5. If you are disorganized, you will trail past your stop time, and no one likes that. Not the audience, the promoter, or the other speakers to follow you.

6. So you don't anonymously blend in with all the other speakers that will come before and after you, you have to create something different that will help you stand out and be memorable.

7. The logical flow of your talk must be tighter than in a longer talk, or your audience will perceive you simply as a five-minute blatherer.

8. Your talk must be better memorized, because you'll have no time to develop it as you go, or to use audience interaction or other speech devices to help you remember your material.

9. You have to "play off of" the previous speaker so you get the audience's attention quickly. If your style is the same as what they just heard, they may easily tune you out.

10. You have to "make the ask", just as in any other length speech. Some wise person said, "There is only one purpose in giving a speech, and that is to get the audience to think differently, feel differently or act differently". Know how you want the audience to change as a result of your time on the platform, and you will very likely hit the mark with them.

BONUS TIP: Many speakers want to "tell everything they know" about a subject. In a day-long seminar, this may be somewhat possible. Never in a speech of an hour length. In a speech shorter than that, it's a disaster. You will never get going and your audience will wonder what just happened. Instead, keep your message to the point, on target and laser-focused.

For every 15 minutes of platform time, the smart, dedicated speaker has spent an hour in development, rehearsal and preparation. It makes a difference. As a famous violinist said, "When I do not practice for three days, my audience can tell. When I do not practice for two days, my orchestra can tell. When I do not practice for one day, I can tell". So it goes with speech making. You want your audience to applaud you, think well of you and act on your message. Doing all that takes some doing on your part.

❝ ❞

Thoughts About Speaking

"The success of your presentation will be judged
not by the knowledge you send but by what
the listener receives."

Lilly Walters

According to most studies, people's number one fear is
public speaking. Number two is death. Death is number
two. Does that sound right? This means to the average
person, if you go to a funeral, you're better off in the
casket than doing the eulogy.

Jerry Seinfeld

"Speak when you are angry—and you will make
the best speech you'll ever regret."

Laurence J. Peter

How To Write An Awesome Speech

Use This Presentation Writing Checklist

This is a fast way to create and organize material for a speaking program. These questions can get your mind working in the right direction. You do not need to follow this chart exactly, nor do you need to use every item. Simply use this to help focus on ways your audience would be interested in what you have to say.

Here we go.

1. Present the problem, situation or issue.

2. Give explicit examples of the issue.

3. State why this is an issue.

4. Show how this plays out as a problem, with examples.

5. Tell a story about this issue people can relate to.

6. Ask a compelling question to engage people.

7. Relate your personal interest in the material.

8. State how this possibly used to be a problem for you, or for clients of yours.

9. State the problems it causes for people.

10. Ask how this affects your audience, and state the effects.

11. Ask how this affects their team, and state the effects.

12. Ask how this affects their parents, and state the effects.

13. Ask how this affects their coaches, and state the effects.

14. Ask how they are dealing with this issue now.

15. Ask how effective their approach is now for this issue.

16. Ask what will happen if they do NOT have a solid strategy to resolve this issue.

17. Ask what have they tried, that failed.

18. Tell the common myths around this issue.

19. Tell the common mistakes people make in attempting to resolve this issue.

20. Speak in modules, with one idea having a start, middle and end.

21. Speak in modules, with one idea having an intro, an example, some humor, a quote, a technique, an exercise and a summary with homework.

22. Present a historical perspective.

23. Present evidence on both sides of the issue.

24. Use a quote highlighting the issue.

25. Use a one-liner highlighting the issue.

26. Tell how this has shown up in the media.

27. Read from an article describing the issue.

28. Use some humor at least every 15 minutes.

29. Ask challenging and stimulating questions.

30. Hold up a book and give a tip from the author.

31. Ask hypothetical questions.

32. Used frequent summarization.

33. Answer a question from a client.

34. Contrast and compare ideas.

35. Read captions off cartoons.

36. Use acronyms.

37. Use mnemonics.

38. Help the audience use what you have told them.

39. Tell how this is talked about in professional journals.

40. Relate a study that highlights the issue.

41. Give them solutions.

42. Show how they can use these.

43. Tell the pitfalls to avoid with your solutions.

44. Drive the entire talk asking them questions.

45. Tell stories and give examples.

46. Help them create personalized learning strategies for the material.

47. Break your content down into bite-sized, digestible chunks.

48. Tell them what you will be covering today, like a table of contents.

49. Give them something to create, on the spot, a thought experiment.

50. Have them do an exercise, alone, with a partner, in a group.

51. Create teams and have a contest to highlight the principles you are discussing.

52. Have them teach each other with the concepts.

53. Demonstrate the right way and the wrong way to perform a technique.

54. Relate your material to an area the students already know.

55. Use teaching aids to speed learning.

56. Use scientific principles in teaching.

57. Use educational psychology principles.

58. Bridge the gap between theory and application.

59. Explain complex, sophisticated concepts in clearly understood ways.

60. Apply this information to the real world.

61. Help the student use the information by creating functional exercises.

62. Help the student become self-aware.

63. List the top five challenges they face around this issue.

64. Give them a self-assessment.

65. Ask them to take a short quiz.

66. Interview an audience member.

67. Act out the wrong way to do something, then the correct way.

68. Use analogies to highlight the issue.

69. Use metaphors to highlight the issue.

70. Use facts to highlight the issue.

71. Use statistics to highlight the issue.

72. Make a suggestion or recommendation they need to take action on.

73. Give them a writing assignment or action plan.

74. Restate your main points.

75. Make a concluding statement.

76. Make a call to action.

77. Give them a challenge.

78. Assign a task or homework.

79. Take questions.

80. Ask them what made the most impact on them in the program.

81. Ask them how they will transfer these ideas to their lives.

So there you have it, a nice long list of ways you can create and deliver a speech. Now go use your creativity to write the most interesting, varied, educational and memorable speech possible, and your audience will be wowed.

" "

Thoughts About Speaking

Political speeches are like steer horns. A point here, a
point there, and a lot of bull in between.

Alfred E. Neuman

The problem with speeches isn't so much not knowing
when to stop, as knowing when not to begin.

Frances Rodman

The best way to sound like you know what you're talking
about is to know what you're talking about.

Anonymous

PRACTICING PRESENTATIONS

Presentation Practice And Preparation Mistakes

How Many Of These 70 Errors Are You Making?

Do you have a specific plan for preparing for your upcoming presentation? Do you tend to "wing it" or prepare casually, haphazardly, in an ad hoc manner? In your due diligence for preparing for a presentation do you use a checklist to help you cover every aspect you can?

There is a saying regarding learning and training. It's not what you don't know that can hurt you. It's what you "don't know that you don't know" that can hurt you the most. This means that many people believe they can simply take a casual approach to preparing for their upcoming presentation, but if they don't know WHAT to prepare for, or HOW to prepare, or what the potential PITFALLS are regarding the harsh realities of a REAL presentation, they are really just engaging in self-delusional sabotage.

The GIGO Principle

People practice incorrectly for presentations every day of the week. They are unfortunately lulling themselves into a false sense of security. Perhaps they don't want to face the hard work that is required to be able to give an excellent presentation, or they just don't have the time to prepare. Regardless, if you do not prepare properly, you will get what you get. Poor preparation results in poor execution. The GIGO formula prevails in two directions. If you prepare well, you will tend to get good results (Good In, Good Out). If you prepare poorly, you will tend to get poor results (Garbage In, Garbage Out).

Confidence Through Competence

Confidence comes from multiple sources, but the number one source is competence. If you know what you are doing, you will feel relieved and secure. There will still be some naturally understandable nerves and some concern about the outcome for the upcoming presentation, but if you have all your bases covered, at the very minimum you will have peace of mind that you did everything you could to prepare. If you prepare very diligently, you will also activate the "overkill principle" of learning and training. You kick the overkill principle into gear when you practice extra long hours. This helps make your skills automatic, and allows you to go on "automatic pilot" once in the actual presentation. When you are the presentation, you won't have to do much thinking and remembering and you will be less prone to feeling nervous. Your extra training will have made you largely immune to the pressure of the situation, and you can masterfully deliver your material, do so in an engaging way, and be more fully present.

Ways People Make Mistakes When They Practice

Here are the various ways people needlessly cause themselves trouble from poor or nonexistent practice procedures. Take a look at this list and compare these items to how you prepare for a presentation.

1. Thinking only weak, inexperienced speakers need to prepare, so you don't practice.

2. Thinking "It'll all come together when it counts", so you don't practice.

3. Simply reading the talk, and not actually doing a full practice run through.

4. Leaving off color markings on your speech notes to indicate dynamics and impact moments.

5. Forgetting that you read your practice notes with your glasses, but won't be using them in the actual speech.

6. You practice a "placeholder speech" as substitute for the real one you will eventually write, and don't practice the real speech.

7. Poor match of formality/informality to your audience.

8. Too many practices, and you become stale and bored and stop paying attention.

9. Practice sessions that are too long, and that tire you out.

10. Practicing without the props and materials you will be using.

11. You place an overemphasis on content, and ignore delivery.

12. You practice only in your head, not out loud.

13. You practice out loud, but not in the volume, tone or pacing you would really use in the presentation.

14. You don't practice with another person.

15. You try to memorize your content, word for word.

16. When you make a mistake, you stop, get flustered, and start over again.

17. You expect to practice perfectly, and when you don't achieve perfection, you get upset.

18. You don't practice at all, because you "don't want to sound scripted".

19. You change your content each time you practice, since you believe in perpetual improvement.

20. You craft content in one full flowing section, rather than breaking it up into chunks, sound bites or stories.

21. You use big words, esoteric words, jargon, acronyms, insider language and other obtuse word forms in order to impress the audience.

22. You don't research carefully enough to match your content to what the audience wants.

23. You assume that the content you wrote is perfect, without checking with anyone else.

24. You read some articles or viewed some videos on presentation Do's and Dont's, and think that should be sufficient to prepare you.

25. You believe that because you had a presentation a few months ago, that particular experience will carry over and keep you in practice for the next one.

26. You figure you are very articulate, experienced and quick on your feet, so you should be able to answer any question the audience throws at you, without practice.

27. You begin your sentences with "So...", "OK...", "Well...", or "Uhhm".

28. You don't record yourself on audio or video.

29. You avoid giving your content to a real person(s) in real time because you are embarrassed, shy or uncomfortable.

30. When you elicit feedback from a coach or friend or family member, you are defensive and argue

against their advice and about what they see and hear.

31. When you receive little or no corrections from your friends and family when they listen to you in a mock presentation, you assume all is well, and that you are ready to present.

32. When you practice, you don't wear the actual outfit you will wear to the presentation.

33. You don't practice or strategize about the ancillary portions of the presentation—how you will act before your talk, after your talk or for "dead time".

34. You don't memorize or know cold your opening content, or your closing content.

35. You don't even have a closing statement.

36. You don't time your content.

37. You don't game out and have contingency plans for any disruptions that may happen.

38. You don't game out and have contingency plans for the range of distracting or hostile audience members you might encounter.

39. You don't do enough research on the company or audience to be able to ask them intelligent questions.

40. You don't practice techniques that help you "stall for time" when given a question you don't know how to answer.

41. You practice while listening to music, or while doing other distracting activities.

42. You practice only in short snippets of time rather than duplicating the actual length of the presentation to come.

43. You don't practice how to get clarification from an audience member if they ask the question badly, or even if you just don't understand it.

44. You don't practice how to handle an audience member who interrupts your program.

45. You spend time practicing only the easier questions, hoping the audience won't ask you challenging questions.

46. You don't take your practice seriously, and instead goof around.

47. You don't practice at the same time of day that your actual presentation will be held.

48. You practice, but you omit the body language portion of your delivery.

49. If it is a telephone or skype presentation, you don't practice over the phone or video.

50. You don't think you'll be nervous once in the presentation, so you don't focus on learning how to control your stress in advance.

51. You harshly and critically judge and evaluate yourself as you practice and that derails your thought process.

52. You don't "warm up" before you begin your presentation practice session.

53. You allow filler words to be present when you practice.

54. You don't practice for the type of presentation format you will face—panel, group, classroom, banquet hall, etc.

55. When you get stuck or freeze on your content in practice, you stop the session and give up for that day.

56. You don't practice looking at "the audience" as you speak.

57. You continuously picture in your mind the disaster scenarios you dread about the upcoming presentation.

58. You don't practice how to stall for time.

59. You speak quicker than you would in a real presentation in an effort to practice more material in a shorter space of time.

60. You eat or smoke while you practice.

61. You don't have any idea how clear and understandable you are, since you don't have anyone giving you feedback.

62. Your practice sessions have no real plan or direction.

63. You practice content without any clear and logical way of transitioning into the next segment.

64. You drive yourself crazy trying to memorize content, word for word.

65. You don't craft stories to support your content, and instead just have data, facts and bullet points.

66. You recite your content from memory, and it is obvious you are doing so, like a bad actor.

67. You goof around while you practice and don't use the same tone you will have in the real presentation.

68. You don't practice, or strategize about how you will enter the presentation room, or leave it.

69. You begin your practice too close to the date of the presentation, leaving no time to get used to any new changes if necessary.

70. You underestimate how nervous you could feel in the presentation once you have other human beings being sitting directly in front of you, having to really deliver.

Remember that how you practice determines how confident you will feel, and how well you will perform once in the actual presentation. If you know these practice and preparation mistakes, avoid them, and instead practice intelligently and with focus, you can almost be guaranteed that you will go into your presentation situations with the peace of mind and confidence. Good luck!

" "

Thoughts About Speaking

A career public speaker is not what I'm called to be.
I'm called to be a critic.

Tony Campolo

I think the key attributes for a good speaker are
someone that's articulate and someone that puts
a fair amount of humour into what they do.

Jo Brand

Lincoln was the greatest speaker and he was
ridiculed for how he looked, you know?

Kevin Costner

Should You Memorize Your Speeches?

How To Learn And Recall Your Speech Material Under Pressure

Ever hear a speaker deliver a talk that sounds odd, but you can't put your finger on why? Do they sound mechanical? Distant and removed? Flat with no passion? Like they're lecturing to an empty room?

They're probably giving a strictly memorized talk.

They are so careful about saying the perfect word, in the exact order they wrote it, they lose their connection with their audience, if they ever had one in the first place.

Speakers usually memorize their talks out of fear that they need to be perfect as a speaker, or from a desire to be very exact in their information, or because they don't really know their material very well. Of course, if they are reading a brief prepared statement, or material that has legal ramifications to the media or other group, that is different. In these cases reading from notes is permissible and understandable.

In general, for most speakers, I suggest you rarely memorize a talk word for word. There are better ways.

Why You Should Not Try To Memorize Your Talk

Your memorized material will almost always come across stilted-sounding and the audience will almost always know you are working from memory. Every audience knows you planned your talk, and will of course accept that, but they don't want a canned version given to them. Other reasons:

1. The written word is vastly different from the spoken word. Therefore, your talk will sound

very odd, and lack punch when the audience hears your material. Some words sound odd when spoken in relation to other words when they can sound fine to your eye when read. Write your material for the ear, not the eye.

2. There is a great risk that you will get hung up trying to follow your memory perfectly and fail or get lost.

3. In an effort to recall the material, you will "go into your head" to find the words, and lose valuable contact with the audience. This is a killer for any audience. Once you lose them, it can be very hard to get them back.

4. You will unfortunately prioritize the words over the passion, and sound flat.

5. There is a chance you will experience more stage fright than if you use other methods of speech delivery. Memorizing a talk is very pressure-inducing. It's asking yourself to be perfect.

There is help though! Try these methods to organize and deliver your speech.

Nine Ways To Recall Your Speech

1. **Use Note Cards.** Many speakers use various sized index cards containing the highlights or order of their speech. You can simply glance down at the cards as you go. Don't read from them. Don't write the speech word for word. Use an outline or key words and use them as a guide. They are unobtrusive in the palm of your hand. Most audiences find these acceptable for most speakers. Caution-at the time you are doing your signature material or content that denotes you as an expert, it is a bad time to refer to notes. This material you should know cold.

86

2. **Use A One-Page Sheet.** An 8 ½ x 11 sheet of paper can contain your speech outline or key modules and will fold up length-wise nicely. You can hold that and refer to it as needed. Again, most audiences find these acceptable for most speakers. Look at Wolf Blitzer on CNN. He uses this all the way through every broadcast. He's a highly paid pro. If he can do it, so can you.

3. **Use Symbols.** On either the index cards or the one sheet, you can mark pictures, numbers, symbols, or anything else that signifies a large chunk of your material (a module, a story, a theme, a progression, an audience exercise). You can recall what each symbol means through practice. You can map out your entire speech using symbols, no words needed.

4. **Use Props.** Each time you hold up a prop to the audience it has a story to tell. You have planned this in advance and can then deliver that unique material.

5. **Have Prompts On The Stage.** Some speakers use stations around the stage that remind them of the next module. You can even set up index cards or props at each stop.

6. **Use Mental Memory Tricks.** You can memorize your entire talk in module form, using an acronym memory-minder. Say you are speaking on stopping young people from drinking and driving. You could organize your talk like this: STOP: S-Stop drinking and driving-why. T-There are alternatives. O-Other people have overcome drinking these ways. P-People live better lives without alcohol. Simply recall the word STOP and use it as a prompt.

7. **Allow Yourself Spontaneity.** Don't bother memorizing or trying to get the words perfect. Instead, once you have the speech well written and well organized, improvise. Allow yourself

freedom to be extemporaneous and creative in the moment and let it flow. The audience will enjoy it more, you will feel relieved, and you may surprise yourself with how you deliver the talk. This is the secret professional speakers use, who have to deliver the same material week after week. This is how they keep the material fresh, and sounding like they are saying it for the first time. The audience loves it, and the speaker stays fresh, and eliminates boredom and burnout. It is critical to remember that in the actual speech in front of an audience no one knows what the script is, so any changes, misses, errors or additions you make in the moment will never be known. Simply carry on as if you meant to say what you said.

8. **Use Your Own Natural Voice**. Say the talk out loud in your office and audiotape it, doing this from memory, BUT in your own words. Let the words flow and don't get stuck on the exact written words. Let YOUR words pop out. As long as the words you choose are close and have the same meaning and impact, you can probably use those. Listen to the tape and you will hear the words that you are most comfortable with.

Stop memorizing your speeches and allow your natural brilliance to shine forth. Your audiences will love you for it.

❝   ❞

Thoughts About Speaking

Always be shorter than anybody dared to hope.
Lord Reading

Oratory is the power to talk people out
of their sober and natural opinions.

Joseph Chatfield

The eloquent man is he who is no beautiful speaker,
but who is inwardly and desperately drunk with
a certain belief.

Ralph Waldo Emerson

AUDIENCE CALIBRATION

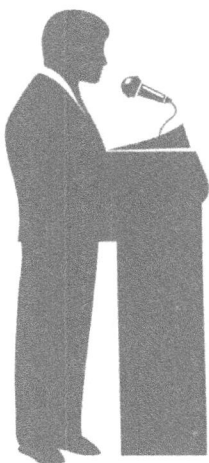

How To Read Your Audiences and Succeed

Understanding The Language Your Audience Speaks

Do you give one-way speeches where you talk and the audience listens? That's called a lecture.

Do you give presentations where you actively interest the audience? That's called an engaging speech.

Do you create persuasive, entertaining and educational programs where the audience comes alive and participates to the maximum? That's called an electrifying happening.

Do you give programs that bore the audience and make them wish they were someplace else? That's called a disaster.

There are many methods to crafting a memorable speech. Many speakers think that once they say their last word, the audience finally has their chance to speak by applauding. But did you know your audience is speaking to you before, during and after your presentation? They speak to you with their body language, their voices, their eyes and their energy. Your job as the speaker? READ this audience language, and react to it.

If you don't read the language the audience is speaking, you will feel a sense of disengagement with them. They will feel it also. Hint--that's a BAD thing!

Some of the worst bad speaker situations I have ever witnessed (as an audience member) were these:

1. The audience began verbally harassing the speaker with catcalls, insults and boos.

2. The audience started to talk loudly among themselves.

3. Some audience members began to balance checkbooks, read newspapers and play computer games.

4. Many people just up and walked out, complaining as they left.

Don't let those happen to you. To have an engaged audience, be engaging.

How will you know when your audience is connected with you, and you are succeeding?

1. They will LOOK interested in you and what you are saying.

2. They will be quiet and listen respectfully.

3. Their faces will seem to light up and smile.

4. Their heads will nod and they will sit up on the edge of their seats.

5. They will sit in an open position, without crossing their arms and legs.

6. They will ask questions and be engaged.

7. They will readily participate in your activities and exercises.

In an ideal world every audience will be interested in you, your material and will want to be there, and engaged in your program. This may happen in part by what they bring to the table, but most of it has to do with you, the speaker. You must read the audience moment to moment and make adjustments in your presentation to suit their needs, moods and desires. You are speaking for THEIR benefit after all, not yours, right?

In what ways can a speaker fail to engage an audience? You can use this as an assessment of your speaking abilities in this regard. Make a check next to any item that you have seen an audience exhibit when you have been speaking. Know these audience interest factors and monitor them as you are speaking. As you calibrate or read your audience you will modify what you do and what you say so you can better meet the needs of your audiences. Do this consistently and your audiences will love you.

43 Ways To Tell If You're Blowing Your Presentation

Now for the harsh realities. How do you know when you are flirting with disaster in a speech? You know you are NOT CONNECTING in your presentation when the audience:

1. Yawns and stretches.

2. Begins to shuffle papers.

3. Rustles, fidgets and moves in their chairs.

4. Appears uncomfortable.

5. Peeks at their PDA's, or cell phones.

6. Appears sleepy and blasé.

7. Seems apathetic.

8. Is staring straight ahead, not following your movements.

9. Seems to have glazed over eyes, as if in a trance.

10. Is rubbing their eyes and touching their face, hands and hair.

11. Looks around the room or out the windows.

12. Begins to sigh and look disturbed and bored.

13. Begins other activities (knitting, reading a book, etc.)

14. Begins tapping their feet, fingers or pens.

15. Begins reading material other than yours.

16. Reads your material and never looks at you.

17. Does not ask very many questions.

18. Is reluctant to answer your questions.

19. Slumps back in their chairs, ready to snooze.

20. Engages in distracting behavior.

21. Does not participate with you or others.

22. Complains about your audio-visuals.

23. Shows limited "agreement behavior" such as nodding heads or smiling.

24. Has a blank or confused look on their faces.

25. Is continuously whispering to each other.

26. Does not laugh at your humor.

27. Does not follow your directions.

28. Interrupts you constantly.

29. Lowers their eyebrows and heads.

30. Looks at their watches or the wall clock.

31. Talks among themselves, and you did not ask them to.

32. Has side conversations off your topic when doing your exercises.

33. Is not taking many notes.

34. Has a bored look on their faces.

35. Avoids eye contact with you.

36. Is sitting back with crossed arms and legs (OK if the room is cold).

37. Does not seem enthused about your exercises.

38. Asks you to explain the rationale for learning your material.

39. Does not come up to you after your talk.

40. Does not get excited about your material.

41. Does not agree with your basic speech premises.

42. Does not agree to do your exercises.

43. Does not buy what you are selling.

So now you know many, many ways audiences respond to dull or irritating speakers. They turn off and they turn you off. As bad as these audience actions are, sometimes things can get worse. Take note.

You know you have ENTERED THE FAILURE ZONE when the audience:

1. Begins eating and drinking and engaging in off-task behavior.

2. Is verbally hostile to you.

3. Heckles or disrespects you.

4. Gives evaluations that are bland, general or negative.

5. Attacks you or accuses you of some bad behavior mid-speech.

6. Falls asleep.

7. Gets up and leaves.

If any of these happen, it's a good bet that you may not be asked back to speak again.

There is no reason you should ever fail in a presentation. Experienced speakers know they can succeed each time because they have so many ways to win, and to help the audience win. Work with a presentation coach to expand your speaker's tool kit and your audiences will treat you with respect and kindness. Lots of applause too.

The bottom line is this. Continually read your audience and make adjustments every step of the way. You will better meet their needs and they will be appreciative of you, the very clever and smart speaker.

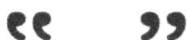

" "
Thoughts About Speaking

Never be grandiloquent when you want to drive home a searching truth. Don't whip with a switch that has the leaves on, if you want it to tingle.

Henry Ward Beecher

Be sincere; be brief; be seated.

Franklin D. Roosevelt

The nature of oratory is such that there has always been a tendency among politicians and clergymen to oversimplify complex matters. From a pulpit or a platform even the most conscientious of speakers finds it very difficult to tell the whole truth.

Aldous Huxley

Are You Making The Speaking Impact You Think You Are?

Do You Know What Your Audience Is REALLY Thinking?

One major goal of every sales presentation you give is to connect with your audience. To help them get something valuable out of your time together. When you give a presentation, do you have ways of checking in with the audience to see how you are fulfilling these goals?

How are they are reacting to your talk? Can you tell if they are bored? Excited? With you? Drifting away? Annoyed? Pleased? Or do you simply roll along with your remarks and assume or hope you are coming across well? Your audience is evaluating their time investment with you by asking themselves some critical questions.

Let's take a peek inside the minds of your audience members to see what they are thinking about your presentation.

The Six Most Critical Questions Every Audience Has On Their Minds

There are six immediately vital questions every audience wants answered in the first few minutes of a presentation. Answer these for your audience and you will start out on a very positive note. Ignore them and watch out!

1. Who is this person and what is in their background that gives them the credibility to speak to us today?

2. What is this talk going to be about?

3. How long will this talk be?

4. Will the speaker help the audience organize the talk so we don't get lost?

5. Why should I listen to this?

6. Will this be interesting, and not a waste of my time?

These are pretty obvious, yet, all audiences are deeply concerned about them. You, the speaker, are responsible for making sure these critical, make-or-break-presentation-questions are answered

Speakers who don't answer these audience questions early and correctly may be faced with these 5 problems:

1. They may fail to connect with their audience.

2. They can alienate people.

3. They will confuse and disorient the audience.

4. They'll lose credibility and impact.

5. Their message will be diluted and ineffectual.

Your audience has additional predictable questions and concerns percolating inside them. With proper planning, you can answer them effectively for your audiences.

1. Will this speaker be easy to listen to?

2. I wonder what they are really like as a person?

3. Will I be called on to participate?

4. Will I be able to ask questions?

5. I hope the speaker tells some good stories.

6. I hope the speaker doesn't over-use numbers, facts and statistics.

7. If they overuse Power point, I am going to fall sleep right in my chair.

8. Will this speaker be using appropriate humor? Will they offend anyone?

9. Will there be any handouts of value?

10. I hope this speaker varies their delivery and technology, so they stay interesting.

11. I hope this speaker can control unruly participants if there are any disruptions.

12. I hope they use vocabulary and examples I can understand and relate to.

13. Please don't let them read the entire talk from notes.

14. I hope they know how to work the A-V technology.

15. I hope this room is not too hot or too cold.

Now you know more about the psychology of how to please your audiences. Be a mind reader when it comes to designing and delivering your presentations so you answer the critical questions your audiences have in their minds. Do that and you'll positively present with more pizzazz, power and profit!

❝   ❞

Thoughts About Speaking

Say not always what you know,
but always know what you say.

Anonymous

A good orator is pointed and impassioned.

Marcus T. Cicero

Why doesn't the fellow who says, "I'm no speechmaker,"
let it go at that instead of giving a demonstration?

Kin Hubbard

The 46 Most Common "Meeting Monsters"

Presenters Encounter

What is your worst nightmare as a speaker, trainer, facilitator or teacher? You're presenting, and you notice that things are not going so well. You realize you are being interrupted, disrupted, distracted, insulted, slowed down, hurried, side-tracked and stymied. Who is doing this? Your audience!

Yes, even though the lights are on during your presentation, you will bump into many scary monsters. Characters. Odd behaving creatures.

Who are these meeting monsters?

These are the folks who annoy, stall, stop and ruin a meeting, speech or team event. They upset your flow as a speaker. They throw a monkey wrench into the meeting works.

Are they odd, weird human beings? Or is this just called the wonderful and mysterious human condition? Guess what? It's normal.

People in your audience bring all their human foibles to every presentation. These personal peccadilloes will arise, to some degree, in every meeting you attend.

People are wonderful, yet they can be challenging in a meeting setting. Group dynamics and historical and current personal psychology are at work, and just because you wish your audience to behave a certain way, there is no guarantee of that happening. Not unless you know what to do when problems arise. And they will arise.

What to do?

First, become aware of these wonderful characters and their ways. Then devise ways to counter their moves.

Your job as the leader (presenter, teacher, speaker) is to recognize these types, have a strategic plan ready, and handle them with tact, diplomacy and aplomb. Then, your meeting will move along smoothly, and you will have mitigated the quirky speed bumps called meeting monsters.

Here are the 46 most typical meeting monsters you will encounter in your presentations. Know them by name.

1. **High Tech Hugh.** He brings a beeper, laptop and an entire collection of electronic gadgetry. He's sad he can't bring more.

2. **Cell Phone Phil.** He's never out of touch with friends.

3. **Cary The Captive.** He is held in class against his will.

4. **Prove-It Pete.** He's a major skeptic who needs proof on everything.

5. **Chit-Chat Charlie.** He never stops talking. It's a disease.

6. **Teacher's Pet Paula.** She is forever trying to make an impression on the teacher.

7. **Silent Sandra.** She won't respond or react to a word you are saying. She's a mystery woman. Check her pulse.

8. **Tommy Turn-Off.** He closes up and turns off. You can't get him to participate in group activities on a bet.

9. **Unsafe Susan.** She's a walking train wreck in group activities. An accident waiting to happen. Make sure you have 911 on speed-dial.

10. **Bored Bob.** All you see of Bob is his open mouth, yawning.

11. **Needy Nancy.** She never seems to have what she needs, and is always asking you to provide for her.

12. **Questioning Quentin.** He asks non-stop questions. And expects answers.

13. **Jerry The Judge.** He passes judgment on everything you do and say, and announces his "findings" to the "court" at will.

14. **High Helen.** By drink or by drug, Helen alters her consciousness.

15. **Take-Over Tim.** Tim tells you how to run the class, give the speech, arrange the room, etc.

16. **Dave The Dominator.** He takes over every discussion and wants to be the boss.

17. **Dumb Question Don.** Don stays awake at night to come up with the most basic, obvious questions he can invent. Then he asks them.

18. **Dan the Doodler.** He thinks he's in art class.

19. **Note Passing Ned.** He thinks he's in junior high.

20. **Hostile Hal.** Hal has a chip on his shoulder, and he dares you to knock it off.

21. **Victor The Volunteer.** He raises his hand for everything. He wants to be involved, always. No one else gets a chance.

22. **Paranoid Patrick.** He feels attacked by everyone and everything. He also attacks back.

23. **Kerry The Caterer.** She brings a seven-course meal to every meeting. Sounds and sights included.

24. **Orville The Offender.** He insults entire classes of people-by race, age, size, gender, religion, etc. He's an all-inclusive, equal opportunity insult artist.

25. **Pop-Up Pat.** She just can't sit still. Every other minute she's out of her chair, going here, going there. Decaf, Pat.

26. **Jeff The Jeweler.** Jeff goes jingle-jangle with his watch, bracelet, necklace, briefcase, pen, pencil and anything else he can grab.

27. **Barry the Bully.** Barry never met a person he couldn't intimidate.

28. **Humorous Helen.** Helen has a joke for every occasion...and will be glad to tell it.

29. **Late Larry.** He never arrives on time. And he's proud of it.

30. **Mark Micro Man.** Mark is a detail freak extraordinaire. He will fuss-budget you to death.

31. **Snoozing Sam.** See Sam sleep. See Sam snore.

32. **Harry the Hurry-Upper.** He's in a rush to get things moving. Or to end the meeting. He'll hurry you, too.

33. **One-Better Ben.** He always can one-up anyone. He has a better idea, a better way, a better comment. He'll share them too.

34. **Yes-But Betty.** She always says "Yes, but..." and then finds 25 reasons to dash your ideas

and suggestions. For Betty, there are no good solutions.

35. **Protocol Paul.** Thinks he co-wrote the book on meeting etiquette, called Robert's Rules. Wanted it named Paul's Rules.

36. **No-Manners Mary.** If Mary can offend, she will. Intentionally or not.

37. **Irene The Indecisive.** Irene is still making her mind up from an event that happened ten years ago.

38. **Side-Talking Tom.** Tom can face straight ahead, yet carry on a side conversation at 90 degrees. He does so often.

39. **Iris The Impresser.** She wants to wow everyone, every time she speaks.

40. **William The Whiny.** He annoys people with his non-stop complaints and troubles.

41. **Carol The Corrector.** Don't worry, if you make even the slightest mistake, Carol will be glad to tell everyone what you did or said wrong. She'll even help you fix it.

42. **Smart-Guy Gary.** He is the original know it all, and he'll tell you so.

43. **Oppositional Ollie.** He plays Devil's Advocate to everything you say. Even if you say nothing. Try it and see.

44. **Side-Issue Steve.** Steve steers the discussion to the left or right, up or down, and sometimes inside or out, anytime he can. He's a regular roller-coaster.

45. **Heckling Hector.** He has a snappy come-back one-liner insult for everything you say. Should

have his own HBO special. Is often mistaken for Don Rickles.

46.   **Hypothetical Harold.** He goes off into La-La Land to invent improbable, impossible scenarios to ask you about. And he expects a straight answer.

How many of these meeting monsters do you recognize? See yourself anywhere in this list? You will never have a room full of "perfect" students or audience members. After all, people are human. They will do what they will, and what they can. Your job as the leader is to recognize these denizens of the deep and respond to them with grace, polish and control so your presentation runs smoothly and you achieve the results you envisioned.

Want to know how to handle each of these characters? Work with a speech coach to create effective measures to counter each move the meeting monsters make. You can do so without appearing to "control" people or the situation. Instead, you'll come off as experienced and savvy, and as a sharp leader who has it all together. Your audience will thank you for it.

❝   ❞

Thoughts About Speaking

Be still when you have nothing to say;
when genuine passion moves you,
say what you've got to say, and say it hot.

D. H. Lawrence

What we say is important... for in most cases
the mouth speaks what the heart is full of.

Jim Beggs

Once you get people laughing, they're listening
and you can tell them almost anything.

Herbert Gardner

GETTING READY
TO SPEAK

41 Peak Performance Questions To Ask Yourself Before You Present

Use this as a pre-program checklist to help you cover your mental preparation tasks. You may find these questions helpful to review weeks in advance of a program. As your presentation date draws near, revisit them and answer them more fully. You may want to write about these in a mental training journal. The better you are able to come to terms with these issues, the more you will be well-prepared and also able to connect better with your audience. You can then deliver a performance that is closer to your potential.

1. ☐ Before my program, do I need to psych up or psych down?

2. ☐ What things should I avoid that tend to psych me out?

3. ☐ What things can I do that will make me feel confident?

4. ☐ Am I taking charge of as much of my pre-program preparation as possible?

5. ☐ What things can I do off-site that will help me connect with my audience better?

6. ☐ On site, before the program, how can I connect with my audience better?

7. ☐ During the program, how can I connect with my audience better?

8. ☐ How soon ahead of my program should I begin preparing mentally?

9. ☐ What last-minute tasks seem to trip me up and get me off-balance before a program? In what ways can I deal with them better?

10. ☐ What people do I need to be around before a program to feel confident?

11. ☐ What difficult people do I need to deal with better before a program so they don't disturb my focus and confidence?

12. ☐ What are some pre-program thoughts I want in my head that will help me prepare?

13. ☐ What are some pre-program self-talk comments I should avoid before a program?

14. ☐ What are some of the helpful mental movies I want in my head before a program?

15. ☐ What are some of the mental images I want to avoid before a program?

16. ☐ What are my favorite and best pre-program nutrition strategies?

17. ☐ What foods and liquids should I avoid before a program?

18. ☐ What are my best pre-program sleep, rest and relaxation strategies?

19. ☐ What technical and stagecraft items should I do far in advance of my program?

20. ☐ Before my program, what music can I listen to that will psych me up, relax me or help me focus?

21. ☐ Before my program, what audios and/or videos of excellent speakers can I experience that will psych me up, inspire me or help me sharpen my mind-set?

22. ☐ What are the time traps that I need to be careful of right before my program?

23. ☐ Who could I enlist in advance to help me reduce stress right before my program?

24. ☐ What sorts of things can I do that put me in a good mood before my program?

25. ☐ What things can I do to partner better with the meeting planner for my program?

26. ☐ What positive things can I do to reduce my stress before a program?

27. ☐ What are the things I should avoid before a program that create stress for me?

28. ☐ What pre-program things can I do that will bring out my enthusiasm and energy during my program?

29. ☐ What outfit can I wear that will make me feel confident and self-assured during my program?

30. ☐ Are there any helpful "superstitions" or "rituals" I can do that will make me feel more secure and organized before my program?

31. ☐ Do I know the opening and closing of my program inside and out?

32. ☐ Have I anticipated the types of questions I may be asked in my program?

33. ☐ Do I have strategies for handling hecklers or uncooperative program participants?

34. ☐ Do I have contingency plans for handling emergencies that may arise in my program?

35. ☐ What signals do my body, mind and emotions give me that I am beginning to prepare to perform the day of my program?

36. ☐ How can I create my program so I can be a more audience-centered speaker?

37. ☐ What are some pre-program strategies that will help me get into the "zone"?

38. ☐ How will I know I am in the zone during a program? How can I stay there?

39. ☐ What process or performance goals can I set for myself, in addition to product or outcome goals?

40. ☐ How fully am I able to give myself permission to succeed in my program?

41. ☐ How well have I come to terms with the paradox of success in my performances?

❝ ❞

Thoughts About Speaking

Broadly speaking, the short words are the best,
and the old words best of all.

Sir Winston Churchill

You can speak well if your tongue can
deliver the message of your heart.

John Ford

What this country needs is more
free speech worth listening to.

Hansell B. Duckett

The 50 Most Common Speech Preparation Errors

How Many Of These Are You Making?

Every speech has a first time. Just don't let it be in front of an audience. That's right. You need to prepare to succeed, and you need to prepare correctly. In my years of coaching speakers, I find many people just don't know what can harm them. I'm not blaming them. They just are not aware. This checklist will make you aware of many of the common ways people self-sabotage when it comes to preparing for a speech, and in giving their program. Use this as a guide for when you create a talk. Use it after your talk as an assessment. Here we go. Which ones have happened to you?

1.   Thinking only weak, inexperienced speakers need to prepare, so you don't practice.

2.   Thinking a spontaneous speech sounds better, so you don't practice.

3.   Not wanting to be "over-rehearsed", so you don't practice.

4.   Thinking "It'll all come together when it counts", so you don't practice.

5.   Simply reading the talk, and not actually doing a full practice run through.

6.   Not planning for emergencies.

7.   Hoping you won't get any tough questions and not planning for them.

8.   Writing the speech for the eyes, and not for the ears of your audience.

9. Printing your talk notes in a font less than 14 point.

10. Writing your speech notes by hand, and then not being able to read them in the actual performance.

11. Not bringing your own light for the lectern, if it will be dark in the room.

12. Leaving off color markings on your speech notes to indicate dynamics and impact moments.

13. Forgetting that you read your practice notes with your glasses, but won't be using them in the actual speech.

14. Rushing your practices, not realizing that everyone rushes even more in the actual speech, due to adrenaline.

15. Not videotaping or audiotaping of your practices.

16. Practicing makes you nervous, so to avoid the bad feelings, you don't practice.

17. You practice a "placeholder speech" as substitute for the real one you will eventually write, and don't practice the real speech.

18. Needing a speech coach, and not hiring one.

19. Calling a speech coach at the last minute to "save you".

20. Writing the talk out word for word.

21. Practicing the talk word for word.

22. Writing the talk at the last minute, and not allowing time for editing and creativity.

23. Writing the speech to impress the audience with how smart you are.

24. Reading from your script.

25. Writing one speech that you try to fit into all speaking situations and for all audiences.

26. Not customizing your speech to the audience.

27. Poor match of formality/informality to your audience.

28. No quiet time before the presentation to focus.

29. Negative thinking and negative expectations.

30. Allowing fear and nerves to get to you.

31. Allowing denial to prevent your practicing.

32. Practicing while you are nervous, so the nerves continue and amplify in the actual performance.

33. Giving so few speeches over time that this particular one builds up in your mind, and creates pressure.

34. Not wearing the clothes or costumes you'll wear in the actual presentation.

35. Not using the A-V tools you'll have in the actual presentation.

36. Sitting while practicing (OK if you will sit while you actually deliver the speech).

37. Reading the talk, without any body language.

38. Rushing the run-through.

39. No enough practices.

40.   Doing partial practices and never running through the entire speech from start to finish.

41.   Too many practices, and you become stale and bored and stop paying attention.

42.   Practice sessions that are too long, and that tire you out.

43.   Practicing without the props and materials you will be using.

44.   Making your only practice session the night before or the morning of your presentation.

45.   Burying your head in your notes and not making any eye contact with your imaginary audience.

46.   Giving an important or brand new speech for the very first time to an important audience, without doing a warm-up speech to a less important audience.

47.   Not warming up the audience, or yourself, by meeting them in advance.

48.   Poor communication with the meeting planner, so you miss and last-minute changes or surprises.

49.   Rushing around and being overly busy the day before or the morning of your speech.

50.   Arriving to the speech venue at the last minute or late.

The first step in reducing and eliminating mistakes is being aware of them. Keep this checklist handy as you prepare for your programs.

" "

Thoughts About Speaking

What you do speaks so loud
that I cannot hear what you say.

Ralph Waldo Emerson

Words ought to be a little wild for they are
the assaults of thought on the unthinking.

John Maynard Keynes

Make sure you have finished speaking before
your audience has finished listening.

Dorothy Sarnoff

Prepare To Speak Your Best

28 Psych Up Strategies For The Platform

Do you have a special psych-up system for getting into the proper mind set for presentations? Do you know how to ready your mind? Do you have a trusted formula that helps you get into the performance zone on a regular basis?

Do you have a system that will keep your mind clear and crisp under pressure?

You want to develop mental readiness strategies so you can prepare with confidence for any speaking situation.

Do you ever wonder why you perform with excellence one day and can't get out of your own way the next? The answer might lie in how you prepare. To fail to prepare is to begin to fail, but psyching up with purpose can light the fire of greatness inside you.

Mental preparation is comprised of long-term preparation (training) and short term preparation (pre-event routines and rituals). Short term mental preparation includes psyching up strategies the day before, the morning of, just before the event and during your program. These four phases are vital to handling performance anxiety, focusing you on your upcoming tasks, keeping you positive-minded and in providing energy to drive your performance.

Easy-To-Use Mental Strategies

Let's now learn about short-term pre-event mental preparation strategies. Here are some approaches I use when coaching business people, athletes and other speakers and coaches.

Everyone has a story about how great preparations lead to great performances. The key is realizing that you have control over how you prepare. Give yourself the gift of psyching up and watch your performances soar!

Athletes, sales people, teachers, public speakers, media people and anyone else who "officially performs" successfully uses pre-performance routines or rituals. You can use routines to help you relax, focus and prepare mentally and physically for an upcoming event. A ritual is a systematic series of steps undertaken prior to the execution of a task designed to help you sharpen mentally, emotionally and physically. You may have things you like to do ahead of your program that make you feel optimistic, confident and energized. This is your ritual. You want to perform tasks ahead of time that contribute to your focus and organization. You should have routines you use to keep you calm, in the proper mood and frame of mind.

Choose Your Speaking Ritual Style

There are two times to use your rituals. One is used for mental preparation just prior to the start of your program and the other is used during the event, but during breaks in the action, to re-focus or re-energize. In addition, there are two broad styles of rituals. If you enjoy focusing specifically on the upcoming event and organizing details, thinking about it, imagining yourself performing well and can see yourself completing the event successfully, you use an associative style of preparation. If doing all that makes you nervous, and you'd rather not focus on what is about to happen, and instead prefer to distract yourself by listening to music, reading, viewing television or the like, then you use a dissociative style of preparation. Both styles are valid and appropriate. The key is to know which one works best for you and to consistently apply that ritual. Remember that even not thinking about the upcoming event is a legitimate style of preparing if you use it consistently across all your performances. This is your customized way of preparing to perform your best.

Ultimately, it may be best to work with a mental game coach to be able to purposively focus on the upcoming event so you can iron out any performance issues and to prepare as fully as possible using the associative approach.

Having a ritual does not mean you are obsessed with its completion. Your ritual exists to serve you, not the other way around. We hear about professional athletes who have superstitious, elaborate rituals they must perform to feel ready to play. We hear of golf pros who may not shave the week of a big event, may eat the same meal at the same restaurant and may wear the same clothes for each round. This is extreme, but it does make them feel secure and confident. Even for professional athletes, the ritual should be easy to perform, take no longer than a few minutes, always be under your control and not require any special equipment. This way you can always perform your ritual.

Powerful Mental Readiness Success Strategies

Here are 28 practical items you can use as a menu for designing your own pre-performance mental speaking rituals:

1.   Eat specific meals at specific times.

2.   Make an overall speaking game plan.

3.   Make back-up and emergency contingency plans.

4.   Check all equipment you will use.

5.   Stretch and exercise to burn off excess nervous energy.

6.   Visualize your success in the program.

7.   Warm-up everything you will use in your performance.

8.   Seek a coach or confidant who will listen to you.

9.   Wear clothes that make you feel confident.

10.   Provide some quiet time for yourself.

11.   Check out the venue where you will present.

12.   Use positive self-talk and positive imagery.

13.   Watch your best performances on videotape, if you have them.

14.   Be around people who support you and make you feel confident.

15.   Be around people who are excellent models of mental toughness.

16.   Know your opening cold so it is automatic.

17.   Read your mental training journal for evidence of past successes.

18.   Maintain a consistent, organized schedule so there is no last-minute rushing.

19.   Seek support staff to reduce pressure on yourself.

20.   Stay tuned to any last minute time or program changes for your event.

21.   Focus primarily on your strengths at the last minute, and leave practicing your weaknesses to your long-term training.

22.   Build up your confidence just before a performance by reminding yourself of the best parts of your program.

23.   Plan your day so as much as possible you avoid stressful situations or conflicts that drain your energy and focus.

24.   Avoid activities that may result in your being tired, depressed or negative.

25.   Continue your usual best schedule of rest, eating, relaxing and exercising.

26.   Avoid over-training and scheduling any last-minute panicky practices that drain your confidence.

27.   Have a game plan so you know what you hope to do once in your program.

28.   Spend time around people who will support your efforts and who validate you.

Rituals are perhaps the most misunderstood and most under-used mental training tools in a speaker's tool kit. If you have experienced hypnosis, relaxation training, autogenics, meditation, prayer, long retreats, yoga or other mind-body disciplines, you can attest to the deep focused relaxation and feelings of well-being that accrue. If you spend time with any top performers you will observe their rituals and routines that propel them out of ordinary consciousness into the hyper-state of intense focus that is required to reach the flow state-- the peak performance state.

To reach your potential on the platform, you have to be able to control your mind. You do that by controlling your rituals.

Begin building your custom mental rituals for out-standing speaking power now.

"   "

Thoughts About Speaking

Many attempts to communicate are nullified
by saying too much.

Robert Greenleaf

Words are, of course, the most powerful
drug used by mankind.

Rudyard Kipling

No one ever complains about a speech being too short!

Ira Hayes

HANDLING
STAGE FRIGHT

Presentation Control Factors

Many speakers become nervous from all they need to do to succeed. They can drive themselves into a state of panic over the endless details required to be successful. In reality, you only have direct control over some of these variables. The secret to stress control is to know which variables you can control, and which ones you should let go.

In this list below you can see that many factors fall neatly into some of the categories, but some do not. This middle, grey area is the area that comprises your ability to exert personal influence over other people in your speaking experience, so as to gain some harmony or leverage. This is difficult to quantify, but it would be just a few percentage points.

Inexperienced speakers, and people who have an unrealistic mental approach to their speaking, focus heavily on the variables that are 100% out of their control. They also attempt to control the variables only partially in their control. They want reality to conform to their wishes and desires. This approach does not work. How can you make changes to things out of your control? Remember, the definition of insanity is doing the same thing over and over, yet expecting different results!

Experienced and smart speakers focus 97% on those variables they CAN control, about 3% on the variables they can partially control, and let the rest go. That's right, they DON'T focus on the items that are out of their control.

Here's how to utilize this material on a practical basis, as you go through your various speaking tasks.

1. I suggest you memorize this list. Probably by now you almost have that done.

2. Keep this list in the back of your mind, and know the various buckets each item falls into as you are engaged in the speaking game.

3. Catch yourself when you whine, complain, feel sorry for yourself, think something is unfair or wish things were different.

4. Learn to let go of these unrealistic wishes and urges about things you can't control.

5. See yourself as a winner, not a whiner.

6. Face reality, and don't hope for a perfect speaking world.

I strongly urge you to memorize this list, and to use it on a daily basis to keep your mind on track on only those things over which you can exert some degree of control.

25 Variables 100% Out Of Your Control

1. Type of presentation.

2. Location of presentation.

3. Presentation room conditions.

4. Presentation city location.

5. Time of the presentation.

6. Date of the presentation.

7. Length of the presentation.

8. Format of the presentation.

9. Number of people in the audience.

10. Number of presentations that day.

11. Noise level of the presentation room area.

12.   Temperature in the presentation room.

13.   Weather that day.

14.   Parking situation.

15.   Traffic on the way.

16.   Disruptions in the presentation.

17.   Who the meeting planner is.

18.   Meeting planner personality.

19.   Questions that are asked.

20.   Questions that are not asked.

21.   Number of questions that are asked.

22.   Audience behavior quirks.

23.   Other presenters, if any.

24.   Where people sit in the room.

25.   Luck.

Six Variables Partially In Your Control

1.   Behavior of support staff.

2.   Other people's expectations for you.

3.   The pace of the presentation.

4.   Whether people like you.

5.   What the audience may be thinking about you.

6.   If you get a standing ovation or not.

The Seven Most Critical Things You Control 100%

1. Your thoughts.

2. Your mental images.

3. Your attention.

4. Your breathing.

5. Your muscles.

6. Your behavior.

7. Your emotions.

27 More Variables 100% In Your Control

1. Your attitude.

2. Your mindset.

3. Your mood.

4. Your stress control.

5. Your rituals.

6. Your answers.

7. Your pacing.

8. Your sense of humor.

9. Your creative thinking.

10. Your self-coaching.

11. Your self-esteem.

12. Your self-image.

13. Your happiness.

14. Your satisfaction.

15. Your affirmations.

16. Your effort.

17. Your strategy and tactics.

18. Your will to succeed.

19. Your reactions to things.

20. Your mental toughness.

21. Your ability to bounce back from set-backs.

22. Your planning.

23. Your decision.

24. Your analysis.

25. Your nutrition.

26. Your presentation practice.

27. Your clothing.

❝ ❞

Thoughts About Speaking

I was dreading winning. I didn't even prepare an acceptance speech. I was worried that I would slip up or do something horrible. I was shaking in my seat, putting on a posed smile. Inside I was petrified.

Leonardo DiCaprio, at the 1998 Academy Awards

My job is to talk; your job is to listen.
If you finish first, please let me know.

Harry Herschfield

Once you get people laughing, they're listening and you can tell them almost anything.

Herbert Gardner

You Are Not Alone
If You Have Stage Fright

What do these famous actors, musicians, writers, scientists, astronauts, TV personalities, politicians, presidents, comedians, inventors and performers have in common?

1. Jason Alexander
2. Neil Armstrong
3. Isaac Asimov
4. Lucille Ball
5. Kim Bassinger
6. Ingrid Bergman
7. Andrea Bocelli
8. David Bowie
9. Erin Brockovitch
10. Roseanne Barr
11. Carol Burnett
12. Robert Burns
13. Nicholas Cage
14. Dean Cain
15. Naomi Campbell
16. John Candy
17. Jim Carrey
18. Johnny Carson
19. Pablo Casals
20. Cher

21.   Agatha Christie

22.   Winston Churchill

23.   Kevin Costner

24.   Courteney Cox-Arquette

25.   Tom Cruise

26.   Winston Churchill

27.   Johnny Depp

28.   Robert DeNiro

29.   Emily Dickinson

30.   Phyllis Diller

31.   Bob Dole

32.   Bob Dylan

33.   Thomas Edison

34.   Albert Einstein

35.   Gloria Estefan

36.   Melissa Etheridge

37.   Sally Field

38.   Harrison Ford

39.   Henry Fonda

40.   Aretha Franklin

41.   Sigmund Freud

42.   Ella Fitzgerald

43.   Calista Flockhart

44.   Robert Frost

45.   James Garner

46.   Richard Gere

47.   Al Gore

48. Ulysses S. Grant
49. Hugh Grant
50. Sir Alec Guinness
51. Gene Hackman
52. Tom Hanks
53. Mia Hamm
54. George Harrison
55. Nathaniel Hawthorne
56. Ian Holm
57. Bob Hope
58. Julio Iglesias
59. Michael Jackson
60. Thomas Jefferson
61. Scarlett Johansen
62. Naomi Judd
63. Garrison Keillor
64. Nicole Kidman
65. Tom Landry
66. John Lennon
67. David Letterman
68. Abraham Lincoln
69. Courtney Love
70. Nancy Marchand
71. Ann Margaret
72. Alanis Morisette
73. Sir Isaac Newton
74. John Cougar Mellencamp

75. John Madden

76. John McEnroe

77. Donnie Osmond

78. Marie Osmond

79. Sir Lawrence Olivier

80. Michelle Pfeiffer

81. Brad Pitt

82. Susan Powter

83. Elvis Presley

84. Burt Reynolds

85. Cathy Rigby

86. Don Rickles

87. Joan Rivers

88. Julia Roberts

89. Theodore Roosevelt

90. Arthur Rubinstein

91. Rene Russo

92. Roy Rogers

93. George Bernard Shaw

94. Barbra Streisand

95. Rod Stewart

96. Carly Simon

97. Willard Scott

98. Andres Segovia

99. Rod Stewart

100. Britney Spears

101. John Stossel

102. Charles Schultz
103. John Steinbeck
104. Dave Stewart
105. Harriet Beecher Stowe
106. Alfred Lord Tennyson
107. Nikola Tesla
108. Carrie Underwood
109. Sigourney Weaver
110. Ricky Williams
111. Oprah Winfrey
112. Orville Wright
113. W.B. Yeats

These famous performers and high achievers have been, or still are, plagued with incredibly debilitating stage fright, performance anxiety or extreme social anxiety (shyness). As you read this list, realize that though they have experienced this malady, they have found a way through it to successfully pursue their craft.

"   "

Thoughts About Speaking

I don't like to hear cut-and-dried sermons.
When I hear a man preach, I like to
see him act as if he were fighting bees!

Abraham Lincoln

When genuine passion moves you, say
what you've got to say, and say it hot.

D.H. Lawrence

You cannot speak that which you do not know.
You cannot share that which you do not feel.

Jim Rohn

AVOID THESE SPEAKING ERRORS

Death By Speaker

What Makes For A Dull And Boring Speaker?

Here Are The 59 Most Common
Audience Complaints

Does any speaker go out of their way to be deadeningly dull? If not, does being a bore just come naturally for some presenters? It appears so. You have no doubt attended more than one speech or meeting where you wish you had stayed home. Or where you were able to catch up on last-week's lost sleep. Or that you were back in Mrs. Migillacutty's terminally-boring junior-high class in English pronouns.

Some speakers could teach the class on "How To Be Dull For Fun and Profit". As one training expert put it, boring should only be for oil drilling companies.

What makes a speaker dull? Here are the 59 reasons audiences give.

1.   Talks about themselves incessantly.

2.   Feigns interest, or has no real interest in the audience.

3.   Gives a book report, material is not engaging.

4.   Gives the audience nothing to do but listen.

5.   No Q and A session.

6.   Poor handouts or none at all.

7.   Does not follow handouts.

8.   Makes no emotional or intellectual connection with the audience.

9. Uses weak humor, or has none at all.

10. Speaks far over or under the knowledge level of the audience.

11. Uses foreign phrases (Latin, French, etc.) that no one understands.

12. Tired, old content.

13. Little or no audience interaction.

14. Tells few stories or none at all.

15. Uses excess data and facts.

16. Uses other people's stories or old ones.

17. Over-uses technology.

18. Speaks too fast or too slowly.

19. Uses too many facts, figures and statistics.

20. Speaks too much to the head and not enough to the heart.

21. Too dry, academic and professorial.

22. Uses too much jargon and too many acronyms.

23. Uses arcane and obscure vocabulary words and phrases.

24. Has annoying and distracting personal habits and mannerisms.

25. Speaks to the educational level of only one audience segment.

26. Makes the talk a lecture and speaks to the audience like children.

27. Does not use words the audience understands.

28. Allows limited or the same people to dominate with questions and comments.

29. Uses the same presentation techniques repeatedly.

30. Uses stories and examples that have no point or relevance.

31. Speaks in a monotone.

32. Uses pet phrases incessantly.

33. Uses inside jokes and material the entire audience does not understand.

34. Leaves out critical content or steps so the speech flow is lost.

35. Poor speech structure and organization makes the talk hard to follow.

36. Can't be heard in the back of the room.

37. Speaks to only a few people in the room, usually in the front.

38. Makes poor or no eye contact.

39. Hides behind the podium.

40. Does not use adult learning principles.

41. Stands like a tree with no gestures.

42. Repeats the same gestures over and over.

43. Uses examples and metaphors the audience can't relate to or understand.

44. Gives information the audience already knows.

45. Gives information the audience does not need or want to know.

46. Continually gets side-tracked.

47. Uses boring and badly-produced media.

48. Uses lack-luster language.

49. Overly-controlling and full of rules for participants.

50. Makes references to obscure, arcane facts and statistics.

51. Has too much dead time between segments and modules.

52. Reads all the words on slides and PowerPoint.

53. Does not know the presentation technology and botches its use.

54. Reads the speech.

55. Overly-focused on minutiae.

56. Is bored and lets it show.

57. Acts self-important.

58. Sells products too often.

59. Acts officious and pompous.

Want to avoid committing these deadly dull and boring speaking sins? For starters, know this list. Then build your speaking repertoire of skills so you have variety, breadth and depth so no matter what else you do, you are not BORING.

Go forth and be dull no more!

“ ”

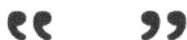

Thoughts About Speaking

The sanity of the average banquet speaker lasts about two and a half months; at the end of that time he begins to mutter to himself, and calls out in his sleep.

James Thurber

We worry about appearing awkward in a presentation. But up to a point, most people seem to feel more comfortable with less-than-perfect speaking abilities. It makes the speaker more human - and more vulnerable, meaning he is less likely to attack our decisions or beliefs.

John P. Kotter

Being a comfortable public speaker, which involves easily being able to go off-script, strongly signals competence.

Amy Cuddy

The 47 Most Common Complaints Meeting Planners Have About Speakers

Having the perfect speaker can make the difference between your meeting being a dream or being a nightmare.

If you hire speakers, you know things can sometimes go wrong, even with the best, most polished speakers. That's why you want to eliminate basic meeting mistakes that just don't need to occur. Hire the wrong speaker, and your headaches will only multiply.

There is a saying, "No speaker is perfect, but when things go wrong at a meeting, an experienced speaker's abilities come to the fore and save the day".

There is another saying, "Smart speakers don't make basic, dumb speaking mistakes". But inexperienced speakers can make dumb mistakes. Those mistakes can be costly. Fortunately, if you hire the right speaker they don't have to be made.

I've witnessed many of these goofs. I was a meeting planner when I was on the Board of Directors for the National Speakers Association in Northern California. I helped hire speakers, promote them, organize their room and AV set-up, introduce them and rate them. I still help clients run their meetings where I speak.

This is what meeting planners and audiences complain about when it comes to speakers who do not know what they are doing. The speaker can make these critical gaffs that can ruin the entire audience experience.

Here are the 47 most common errors speakers can make before, during and after a presentation.

1. Little or no research on the audience's needs and wants.

2. Little or no understanding of the meetings industry.

3. Little or no understanding of the audience's industry.

4. Doesn't understand the meeting objectives.

5. Doesn't understand their role in the meeting.

6. Shows up late or at the last minute.

7. No room or AV preparation.

8. Gets in the way of the meeting planner.

9. Fails to meet and greet the audience in advance.

10. Fails to create rapport with the audience.

11. Unavailable by phone, fax or email.

12. Demanding and big ego.

13. Inflexible when problems come up.

14. Unprofessional behavior and image off-stage.

15. No interest in meeting the people in your organization off-stage.

16. Unethical behavior.

17. No coordination of message with prior speakers.

18. Insults the audience through sex-ism, gender-ism, class-ism, age-ism, race-ism, size-ism, etc.

19. Insults the audience, sponsors or meeting planner.

20. Gives a book report, not engaging material.

21. Fluff-based content, with no real research or meaningful data.

22. All style and no substance.

23. Gives an off-the-shelf talk when a custom speech was promised.

24. The audience does nothing but sit.

25. Few or no audience interaction techniques.

26. Falls victim to stage fright.

27. Has no Q and A period or handles it poorly.

28. Poor handouts or none at all.

29. Makes no emotional or intellectual connection with the audience.

30. Doesn't support the meeting themes and messages.

31. Uses weak humor, or has none at all.

32. Inappropriate, insulting use of humor.

33. Speaks far over or under the knowledge level of the audience.

34. Tired, old content.

35. Tells few stories or none at all-they are nothing but data and facts.

36. Uses other people's stories or old ones.

37. Uses content that is not applicable to the audience's challenges.

38. Does not help the audience transfer the speech material to their particular pragmatic needs.

39. Lack of respect for audience members.

40. Not ADA or OSHA aware or compliant.

41. Under-uses or over-uses technology.

42. Sells product when inappropriate.

43. Does not take leadership, especially in an emergency.

44. Leaves immediately after the presentation.

45. Does not clear the stage quickly for the next speaker.

46. Does not speak with the meeting planner, post-talk, for feedback purposes.

47. Takes the check and runs.

Speakers who make mistakes like these can ruin a meeting. They may be all about themselves, and have demanding egos. They may simply be inexperienced. They may have low awareness of how to make a meeting special. Worse, perhaps they don't even care.

Whatever the reason, it's important to hire experienced speakers who provide a "pledge of services" so you know what you are getting.

Hire the right speaker and your meeting nightmares will be replaced with sweet dreams.

❝   ❞

Thoughts About Speaking

I think the power of persuasion would be
the greatest superpower of all time.

Jenny Mollen

In making a speech one must study three points: first,
the means of producing persuasion; second, the
language; third the proper arrangement of the
various parts of the speech.

Aristotle

Ninety percent of selling is conviction,
and 10 per cent is persuasion.

Shiv Khera

15 Fatal Flaws Inexperienced Speakers Make

Avoid These Platform Gaffs
And Start Presenting Like A Pro

When you sit and watch an experienced professional speaker take hold of an audience, you are seeing magic in action. They make everything look so easy and smooth, you wonder, "Were they born with a silver microphone in their mouth?"

In actuality, all that platform polish comes with the price of many years of hard work and training. That's how they make everything come off with such seeming ease. They've paid their dues many times over.

If you are less experienced than you'd like to be, you probably make some errors in speaking that could be easily fixed. If you just knew what they are!! I want you to know the most common speaking mistakes that people new to speaking make. Once you know these, your confidence and effectiveness as a speaker will multiply many fold.

Here we go, the 15 most common speaking gaffs speech-givers make.

1. STOP arriving to your program at the last minute so even you wonder if you are going to make it on time. What do you suppose this does to the audience and organizers who are stressed out from not knowing if they will have a speaker?

2. STOP playing fast and loose with the clock. You can't simply start and stop your talk on your own terms. The organizers have a schedule to keep and your audience wants to be respected for their valuable time as well. Stay on

schedule, and preferably, stop a bit earlier than you said you would to take questions.

3. STOP jumping into your talk without attempting to gain some rapport with your audience. All audiences need to be warmed up, and taking the time to do this can help you give a better performance as well.

4. STOP trying to "wing it" by making up your talk as you go, and "speaking from experience". Professional speakers don't even do this, so don't think you can get away with it. The audience will know.

5. STOP being so theoretical, conceptual, intellectual and statistical. These are all guaranteed to turn off any audience and turn them against you. People want practical, useable material they can apply to their lives and careers, not heavy academic, jargon-laden content that requires a Ph.D. to understand.

6. STOP trying to be all things to all people as you speak, by wandering all over creation in an attempt to be "comprehensive" or a "renaissance person". You'll simply confuse people, who will be wondering what your topic is, and why they came to your program.

7. STOP dressing like you just came from a beach party or a backyard barbecue, or like you are on the way to the hairdresser. Audiences like their speakers to look sharp, professional and well put together. At the minimum, a well-kept look gives you extra points on credibility before you even open your mouth. First impressions count.

8. STOP using the same speech for every audience. Do audience research and customize your talks. Your audience will really appreciate that and probably ask you back for more. You

at least will be speaking their language and hit the mark better than with a canned presentation.

9.   STOP assuming that all your audiovisual equipment and room has been set up properly by someone, or that nothing has changed since you last touched it. This is the stuff of disasters, and something you can easily avoid.

10. STOP negating the value of solid writing, platform and staging skills. Every audience deserves the best speaker they can get, and you have an obligation to continue improving on your speaking skills every year.

11. STOP boring the audience. Enough said?

12. STOP overwhelming the audience with too much, or unnecessary information they don't want or need. If you do your homework, you'll know what will please them.

13. STOP teasing the audience by being miserly about how much detail you are willing to give in your content. Some speakers say to the audience, "I won't give you that information, because it's in my book". Perhaps some audiences might be thinking, "I won't be giving you my money for your book".

14. STOP using insensitive, negative, disrespectful and uninformed jokes, stories, remarks, news events and other content that will alienate your audiences, unless you have a good lawyer on retainer.

15. STOP displaying such a big ego. Remember, speaking is all about the audience and their needs, not the speaker's gratification.

I know now you will START planning better, crafting your speech better and staging and delivering your speech with more attention to the needs of the audience. I also know you will STOP making any more of the 15 fatal flaws we just reviewed.

Enjoy your speaking. Your audiences will really appreciate the new you! You just moved your speaking skills up a complete level!

❝   ❞

Thoughts About Speaking

Selling is a natural skill. It's developed as a child.
You may know it as persuasion.

Jeffrey Gitomer

Not brute force but only persuasion and faith
are the kings of this world.

Thomas Carlyle

The object of oratory alone in not truth, but persuasion.

Thomas Babington Macaulay

The 23 Most Common Vocal Mistakes Presenters Make

You probably have attended a presentation where the speaker was quite difficult to listen to, but you couldn't put your finger on why. Another time you were enthralled by a wonderful speaker. They truly pleased you. Again, you didn't know why. What's the difference here? Very likely, it's the speaker's voice.

Some speaking voices require conscious mental effort to be understood and to be listened to for longer periods of time. Extreme effort must be expended to grasp the words, and overall, the voice is not pleasing to the ear. It's much like going to a concert and finding that while all the notes are being played "correctly", something is still wrong.

Conversely, some speaking voices are straight from heaven. They seem almost musical, with the ability to vary the pitch, tone, volume, accent, energy and power at will. These are the virtuoso voices we could listen to all day.

For most speakers, voice usage is one of the last areas of improvement. Fortunately, though, there is help. The first step? Become aware of what is. Then you'll have the power to create change.

This is a list of the 23 most common mistakes public speakers make with their vocal delivery. Audiences complain about these incessantly.

1.   Squeaky and high-pitched voice.

2.   Speaking too fast.

3.   Speaking too slow.

4. Using jargon and unfamiliar terms.

5. Accent that can't be understood without great effort.

6. Poor word choices and poor grammar.

7. No natural flow of thoughts, or poor logical order.

8. Not enough white space (pauses), regardless of speaking speed.

9. Too much white space, stopping the flow.

10. Thinking out loud, using a stop-start style.

11. Using run-on sentences that never seem to end.

12. Ending sentences with the voice going upward, as if asking a question.

13. Mumbling and imprecise diction.

14. Volume too low.

15. Volume too high.

16. Little or no variation in vocal delivery.

17. Pressured speech, where words come out in a torrent.

18. Breathy, airy and soft tone.

19. Nasal tone in voice.

20. Tripping over certain words.

21. Using words not suited to the ear of listeners (Speech writing is for the ear, not the eye, as in reading).

22. Flat and monotonic pitch.

23. Low energy and lifeless, with no enthusiasm.

It is not a requirement that a speaker lose a regional or international accent. They don't need to adopt the "TV anchor" style of accent-neutrality we hear on the airwaves. I have enjoyed listening to speakers with quite "heavy" accents, but they have modified their speaking so everything they said was easily understandable.

The important basic key is to make the speaking voice "irritation free" so listeners can readily enjoy themselves. This is a minimum requirement. To next raise the voice performance to a higher level, the speaker would then begin to use the voice musically to create certain experiences for the audience. These would be:

- Suspense and drama

- Quieter, softer moments

- Rousing and exciting times

- Humorous episodes

Your first step in improving your speaking voice is to be aware of these lists. Then record yourself when you speak. Ask friends and a speech coach for their opinions. Practice modifying your voice usage and quality and eventually you will create the speaking voice that is not only pleasing to audiences, but is an effective tool for getting your message across with power, dramatic effect and credibility. Audiences will eagerly respond to your message more positively and with greater appreciation.

❝ ❞
Thoughts About Speaking

Education's purpose is to replace an empty mind
with an open one.

Malcolm Forbes

Anyone who stops learning is old, whether 20 or 80,
anyone who keeps learning stays young. The greatest
thing in life is to keep your mind young.

Henry Ford

An education isn't how much you have committed
to memory, or even how much you know. It's being
able to differentiate between what you do know
and what you don't.

Anatole France

The 44 Most Common Mistakes Speakers Make With Their Body Language

Ever see a speaker behave a certain way on stage and react negatively to it? Perhaps you can't even articulate what it is they did, but you know something was "off". Their behavior did not match what they said. There was an incongruence. A dissonance. A lack of integrity between their words and their behavior.

When you witness a speaker exhibiting this body-mind mismatch, it throws the entire presentation into a tailspin. Something just feels wrong. The audience feels uncomfortable and the speaker loses credibility with their message.

What is this strange phenomenon?

Body language. Non-verbals. The unspoken part of the speaker's message. It's estimated that only 5-10% of a speaker's message is received by the audience through the speaker's words. Another 30-40% is received through the sound of the voice. A whopping 50-65% comes across from the speaker's body language.

Yes, the non-verbals a speaker possesses can make or break them. Credible or false. Confident or scared. Original or a copy. Leader-like or just faking it.

Body language can be analyzed, re-directed and learned to a degree that makes the mind-body connection credible or natural. That takes practice and that's for another time. The scope of this discussion is to bring to your awareness the many types of body language errors speakers make in the course of a presentation.

The audience reactions described here may not happen every time, but are often typically negative, in response to a speaker's physical gaffs on stage. Be conscious of these the next time you present or see a speaker on stage or TV.

1. **The Arm Crosser.** The speaker stands with arms across the chest. This can make them appear to be almost protective or pompous. The audience reacts by retracting emotionally.

2. **The Ice Skater.** The arms are held behind the back, much like an Olympic speed-skater. The audience wonders what the speaker is hiding back there, and why they don't gesture.

3. **The Swayer.** The speaker stands in one spot, but tilts from side to side, in nervous fashion. The audience begins to get sea-sick.

4. **The Rock Star.** The speaker moves from weight backward to weight forward, like on a swing. The speaker look nervous, and the audience feels that fear.

5. **The Toe Popper.** While speaking, the presenter repeatedly pops up onto the toes of each foot simultaneously, and appears to grow 2 or 3 inches in height each time. The audience is distracted watching this athletic display.

6. **The Lock-Body Head Turner.** As the speaker turns to point to something (a screen, slide, or audience member) only their head turns. The rest of the body is locked into place. The audience can tell there is fear locking up the body.

7. **The Note Eater.** The speaker buries their head down into their notes, as if to eat them. The audience really wants to see the face of the speaker.

8. **The Lectern Wrestler.** The speaker has a grabbing contest with the lectern, out of fear. The audience thinks the speaker is steadying his nerves.

9. **The Hypnotized Screen Reader.** As the slides appear on the screen, the speaker is mesmerized, reading each caption word for word. The audience begins catching up on their sleep.

10. **The Hitch-Hiker.** The speaker uses his thumb to point at the slides. The audience begins looking for traffic.

11. **The Finger Pointer.** The speaker uses his finger to point, and the audience reacts by feeling accosted.

12. **The Paper Clutcher.** The speaker just can't let go of their notes. They carry them everywhere. The audience wonders why.

13. **The Microphone Mangler.** The speaker holds the microphone oddly-- either too low, too high, too close, too far or too tight. The audience marvels at the show.

14. **The Podium-Pounder.** To make a forceful point, the speaker slams the lectern with his fist. The audience shrinks back as they hear the feedback from the microphone.

15. **The Camouflage Speaker.** The speaker hides behind whatever they can find--the lectern, AV equipment, a microphone stand. The audience wonders what the disappearing act is all about.

16. **The Coin Seeker.** The speaker unconsciously fishes for coins in his pocket for stress relief, never pulling any out, but makes enough noise to have the audience focusing on the coins over his voice.

17. **Hands In Pocket.** The speaker feels relaxed and casual with both hands in his pockets. Audience members see him as bored, tired and aloof.

18. **The Toy Player.** Pens, ties, pointers, slides, keys, coins, paper clips and all else within reach are fair game for the speaker who likes to play with toys as they speak. The audience plays along too--by watching the toys rather than the speaker.

19. **The Jewelry Smithy.** Jewelry can be beautiful works of art. It can also be noisy and flashy, and the audience will be distracted.

20. **The Figleaf Lover.** The speaker holds both hands in front of the crotch area, in a very passive and cliché-ridden pose. The audience feels like they are at the Gong Show.

21. **The Fist Clencher.** With one or both fists tight, the speaker sends the message of anger or fear. The audience receives it loud and clear.

22. **The Eyeglass Tilter.** Because his glasses are not centered perfectly, the speaker continually adjusts them. This is not something the audience ignores.

23. **Peripatetic Pete.** This speaker never stands still for a moment. They walk all over the stage while the audience tries to follow them.

24. **The Barber.** Because appearance is important, or from nerves, the speaker plays with or smoothes his hair every few minutes. The audience rightly interprets this move as either arrogance, nerves or vanity. Maybe all three.

25. **The Robot.** The word "stiff" rises to new heights as the speaker acts robot-like by tightening his body and standing still. The

audience picks up on this and is equally ill-at-ease.

26. **The Animator.** Perhaps there was a good price on extra-strong coffee recently, and the speaker stocked up. Here, movements are fast, wild and distracting. The audience feels tired from trying to keep up.

27. **The Late-Comer.** The speaker makes his point verbally, only to follow with a "perfect" mannerism, but a few beats late. This has the "skipping frame look" of an old silent movie, and the audience begins checking their eyes.

28. **Frenetic Freddy.** Everything the speaker does is rushed. They seem to be in a hurry, and the audience feels swept along by a tidal wave.

29. **The Pacer.** This speaker walks back and forth in the same place so much, they wear a rut into the floor. Must be tiring too. At least the audience thinks so.

30. **The Preener.** Unseen tuffs and specks of clothing lint just must be removed by the speaker. The audience obeys by watching the lint more than the speaker.

31. **The Cowboy.** Just as in the old western movies, the speaker stands with both thumbs in his front pockets. All he needs is a strand of hay sticking out of the side of his mouth. The audience begins looking for the Lone Ranger.

32. **The Politician.** The audience thinks they must be at a political rally, since the speaker is holding both his jacket lapels as he talks.

33. **The Broadway Choreographer.** There is a grand display of affectations and flourishes as the speaker broadly and self-consciously gestures to the maximum. The audience

wonders if there was a parade and they missed it.

34. **The Compulsive Gesticulator.** This speaker has a body movement for almost every single word or phrase they utter. It makes them look contrived and forced. The audience feels manipulated.

35. **The Mis-Matched Mover.** The speaker makes flawless gestures, at the correct time--but they are the wrong ones. For example, the speaker says, "I am very happy to be here tonight", yet frowns and crosses his arms. The audience gets the "real" message.

36. **The Mis-Sized Mover.** The speaker makes gigantic gestures with only a small audience, yet makes minuscule movements in a large hall with a huge attendance.

37. The mismatch makes the audience wonder if they need to be there at all.

38. **The Eye-Rubber.** The speaker begins rubbing his eyes, as if he is tired. The audience actually IS tired from seeing this.

39. **The Genie-In-The-Bottle Move.** The speaker holds both palms together, in front of the body and proceeds to rub them together, back and forth. The audience is waiting, but there is no magic.

40. **The On The Spot Speaker.** This speaker finds a location they like, and they stick to it-- forever. The entire talk comes from one place. The audience wonders if the speaker's feet have gone on strike.

41. **Looking Down The Nose.** The speaker wears his reading glasses low on his nose, looking down at his notes. Some speakers don't even

need glasses to do this. The audience feels like he is looking down on them.

42. **The Face Toucher.** The speaker's entire face seems to need to be touched, because the speaker is continually placing hands on every inch of it. The audience begins watching and wondering and loses track of the words.

43. **The Strutter.** The speaker pompously lopes along the stage, almost as if to say, "Look at how important I am". The audience is thinking, "I don't THINK so".

44. **The Hide-A-Body Angler.** The speaker never fully faces his audience, using only his head or upper body, while standing away from the audience. The sideways stance is puzzling to the audience, and they look at HIM sideways.

45. **The Remote Speaker.** If they could, this speaker would give their speech by telephone. As it is, they hide far in the rear of the stage and create a frosty long -distance relationship with their audience.

Now you should be much more aware of the many physical quirks, excessive posing, body messages and nervous mannerisms that can befall a speaker. The less experienced the speaker, the more odd moves they display. The more experienced the speaker, the smoother, more coordinated and more natural they appear. Hence the term, "polished performer". All the rough edges have been removed.

To improve your physical mannerisms, first be body aware, then re-work your moves so finally, you can appear on stage with a polished and natural style that is a pleasure to witness. Your message will be easier to hear. Your entire presentation will carry more gravity. Most important of all? You'll be more credible. You'll make the very positive audience impact you intentionally set out to create in the first place.

" "

Thoughts About Speaking

Well-timed silence hath more eloquence than speech.

Martin Fraquhar Tupper

Talk low, talk slow, and don't talk too much.

John Wayne

Extemporaneous speaking should be practiced and cultivated. It is the lawyer's avenue to the public

Abraham Lincoln

BUILDING CONFIDENCE IN SPEAKING

Improve Your Public Speaking Confidence

10 Simple Tips To Reduce Your Fears Of Giving A Speech

You probably know the statistic about speaking in public being the number two fear everyone has in life. The number one fear is death. I used to have the fear of dying WHILE giving a speech. That's pretty bad. But I overcame that phobia by determined practice, diligent study and many, many actual speeches.

If you have the desire to conquer your speaking fear, I firmly believe you can do it. Few people had it as bad as me. I would sneak out of high school English class the day we had to give speeches. Now, I speak on the pro circuit. How'd I make that shift? Read on and discover my 10 secrets to speaking confidence.

10 Ways To Boost Your Speaking Confidence

1. **Confidence Through Competence.** People can tell you how good you look and sound, but if you are not confident on the inside, all that talk is simply blather. To prove to yourself that you can do it, you HAVE to DO it, and do it WELL.

2. **Over-Practice Until Things Are Instinctive.** Winging it and speaking on the fly sound exotic and natural, but they induce fear. Rehearse until you are positive you know what you are doing. Then do it again and again until it's ingrained.

3. **Build Rapport Before The Speech Begins**. Nothing is as scary as walking out to speak to a room full of strangers. Make some friends in the audience ahead of time by meeting people before your talk.

4. **Get Some Presentation Coaching.** Cognitive, book knowledge about speaking is not the same as personal awareness of yourself AS you speak. A coach can help be a feedback mirror for you and raise and validate your confidence.

5. **Do Your Homework On The Engagement.** Know your venue, your meeting organization, your audience and your reason for speaking. The more you know, the less you will fear.

6. **Confidence Begets Confidence.** Speak often, and successfully. Even if you speak at lower level, less pressured engagements, these will give you an opportunity to get in your groove.

7. **Know Your Opening And Closing Cold.** The start and finish of any speech are the most nervous times, because you want to make and leave a good impression. Memorize these so you can rattle them off in your sleep.

8. **Center Yourself.** Learn some stress management, particularly the technique known as centering. Stand tall, good posture, relax your mind and begin breathing slowly and deeply. Do this even during the speech itself.

9. **Build In Audience Tasks.** Take the focus off yourself and create moments to catch your breath by giving the audience activities related to your material. This can make your talk more interactive, saving you from having to memorize a full, formal speech.

10. **Have Emergency Plans Ready.** Something can always go wrong in a program, so have contingency plans for accidents, malfunctions, disruptions and all else that can go south. Build in some peace of mind in advance.

You've no doubt heard the "speech tip" that "the audience does not want you to fail...they're pulling for you". Well, I've got news for you. Audiences want you to succeed not because they love you unconditionally. Like any of us, they're a self-focused lot. They don't want you to fail because if you do, that means you just wasted all of their valuable time! So the audience is not some enemy that you must conquer, but you had better know your material, and know what you're doing, or they just might take you and your speech unkindly.

I want you to succeed every time out. Take time to know these ten tips and remember the story of the young man lost in New York City who stopped another man on the street and asked, "How do I get to Carnegie Hall? The man replied, "Practice, my friend, practice!"

" "

Thoughts About Speaking

To be a person is to have a story to tell.

Isak Dinesen

Speak clearly, if you speak at all; carve every word
before you let it fall.

Oliver Wendell Holmes

The most precious things in speech are the pauses.

Sir Ralph Richardson

How To Eliminate Speaking Jitters

Eight Sure-Fire Strategies To Help You Be More Natural On The Platform

Do you avoid giving speeches because the stress drives you up the wall? Do you give speeches, but hate every minute of it? Do you speak well, yet are held back from reaching your potential from the fear and self-doubt you experience?

There is help for anyone who suffers from stage fright. Here are a few of my favorite stress-stopping techniques for speakers.

1. **Don't Call Your Event "A Speech". Instead, Frame The Talk As A Coaching Session, Workshop Or Class.** Why? "Giving a speech" feels like a big deal, pressure-packed situation. Also, few audiences want to spoken to or at by a "speech maker", but almost everyone enjoys the spirited give and take of a conversation.

2. **Use The Overkill Principle, From Sports And School.** If you have a school test or sports competition coming up, what made you feel relatively comfortable and confident going into the event? Overdoing your preparation with extremely hard practice and training. If you barely practiced, you had a genuine reason to be very nervous--you were NOT ready! The same is true for a speech.

3. **Set Speaking Sub-Goals.** A speaking event should also be a learning experience for you, the speaker. One major goal, is of course, to please, motivate, educate and move the audience. Try some new things, take some risks and make sure YOU learn from the event.

4. **Practice All The Time, In Every Venue Imaginable.** Use your speech material as you have casual conversations with people the weeks before your talk, in the coffee shop, lobby, stores, malls, etc. They won't know you are practicing your speech. You'll be able to practice the pronunciations, phrasing, inflection, timing, jokes and all else, just as you will do it from the platform.

5. **Wear Your Most Confident Outfit And Accessories.** Go ahead, be superstitious. Wear what makes you feel good, natural and energetic. Stay away from outfits that lower your self-esteem and confidence level. To be confident, look confident. Simple to do, but powerful.

6. **Accept That Nervousness Is A Natural Part Of Any Performing.** Long time well-known performers across many venues STILL get very nervous before their performances, yet they manage to give very creditable performances, time and again.

7. **You Can Perform Well And Be Very Nervous, Yet The Audience Will Never Know.** You can be terrified inside, but if you go about your speaking, you can completely hide your fear from the audience. The few ways the audience will have hints that your nerves are appearing are when your voice continually cracks, your hands, arms and legs shake visibly or you stutter and stammer (assuming you don't do that naturally). Aside from that, they may never know. Act as if you are confident, and quite often, you will begin to feel confident.

8. **Make The Audience Do Some Of The Work.** Instead of YOU speaking the entire time, give your audience some tasks. Ask them questions,

give them a quiz, have them discover answers to tasks in small groups. Not only will the audience be more engaged and learn better, but you can take a break and gather your thoughts as they do their "homework". Try it, you'll like it.

Remember, even top speaking pros get nervous before and during their speeches. Collect stress-busting strategies like these. Observe experienced speakers and see what they do to reduce their nerves. Embrace your stress and it will serve you well.

"   "

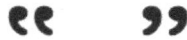

Thoughts About Speaking

True eloquence consists in saying all that is necessary,
and nothing but what is necessary.

Heinrich Heine

Acting is merely the art of keeping a large group of
people from coughing.

Sir Ralph Richardson

The secret of success is sincerity. Once you can fake
that you've got it made.

Jean Giraudoux

The Art Of Speaking

Winning The Mental Game Of Presenting

How many of your speeches could be considered in the artistic category? Do your audiences view you as a master speaker? What would you have to do to boost your speaking to the next level?

Highly experienced speakers not only know their subject, they know themselves, their audiences and their craft. They know how to write, stage and organize winning presentations that engage the audience at all levels.

To kick your speaking up a notch, take any of these 13 tips on as a project and watch your investment in yourself as a speaker grow.

13 Strategies For Making Your Speeches Masterful

1. Go beyond telling your audience about your subject. Be passionate and become engaged with your subject.

2. Demonstrate your credibility and your right to be on the platform by recounting your experiences as an expert and how you solved problems and helped people and organizations.

3. Masterfully customize your material for each audience so they know absolutely that you are there for them.

4. Refine your voice control and turn your throat into a musical instrument your audiences love to listen to at length.

5. Speak from your heart and touch the hearts of your audience. Take risks by being vulnerable, imperfect and your audience will see you as a

real human being, as one of them, not just as "the speaker".

6. Speak the truth and your audience will respond. Avoid any inconsistencies or incongruencies between your "real life" and your "platform life".

7. Tell more stories and give fewer statistics. Reduce the PowerPoint and get more personal and people will respond eagerly.

8. Connect with your audience, one person at a time. Begin the personal touch before you take the stage by "being with" people in the audience, not "talking at" them.

9. Have fun as you speak and so will your audience. To get in the fun mode, stop focusing on yourself, and instead be audience-centered.

10. Respect your audiences and they will respect you. Never insult or disrespect anyone in your audiences. Show your regard for everyone.

11. Stop writing your speeches and start living them. Find your best material from your travels, your work, your friends, your family and the real world around you.

12. Create multi-media presentations to engage people the way they are used to, with modern media. Coordinate your talk points with particular moments in the media show and you will WOW people.

13. Create and deliver your talk from the A-V-K matrix. This means your talk should be approximately 25% auditory, with 45% visual and 30% kinesthetic. You want to speak to everyone's learning styles in the audience.

Now you have a better idea how master speakers make it look so easy. The hard work is in the preparation and in the crafting of the message. Enjoy your journey in the speaking world and you will reap the many benefits of this exciting calling.

❝   ❞

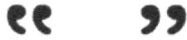

Thoughts About Speaking

The secret of success is learning how to use pain and pleasure instead of having pain and pleasure use you. If you do that, you're in control of your life. If you don't, life controls you.

Tony Robbins

As a child, I loved being onstage. I loved singing, I loved the lights, I loved the adrenaline. I even loved learning lines. I was completely obsessive.

Emma Watson

Eloquence is the poetry of prose.

William C. Bryant

Playing The Mental Game of Self-Coaching For Anyone Who Presents

Top performing professional speakers regularly look for help from coaches, gurus, peers, books and other sources. But all the information in the universe won't help if it's not translated into useable form. This is where self-coaching takes center stage. Self-coaching is the ability to combine knowledge about yourself with outside information to make meaningful, positive changes in your life and to perform well when you need it most.

No one can teach you anything. Ultimately, only you can take information from a teacher or coach and transform it into your personal power. Savvy speakers take responsibility for their own learning and devise strategies and systems that put information into action.

Here are five mental game success secrets that peak performing speakers can use to improve their self-coaching skills.

1. **Be Willing To Grow:** If you are reading this content about self-coaching it means you want to grow as a human being. This desire is manifested by your seeking experiences that help you improve personally, as well as professionally. The self-coaching speaker realizes that to grow professionally, personal growth is a must.

2. **Cultivate A Beginner's Mind:** The Zen tradition says, to learn, we must be an empty vessel. If we know it all, we can't be very open to new knowledge and experiences. The self-coaching speaker realizes that an open, seeking

attitude allows new experiences to come into our consciousness.

3. **Benefit From Mistakes**: Peak performers respect mistakes and use them to learn. Poor performers tie themselves up with negative emotion after every mistake. When we view any mistake as failure, our self-destructive emotions mask the valuable feedback around every mistake. The self-coaching speaker welcomes all feedback.

4. **Develop High Self-Awareness:** Self-awareness is not about what should be-it is about what is. The self-coaching speaker places a high priority on becoming self-aware and realizes that self-knowledge can be about the past or present. Self-awareness is the master skill.

5. **Deconstruct Your Personal Experience:** Peak performers use self-reflection to deconstruct their experiences. They know that the unexamined life fleets by out of control. Only by reviewing personal experience do we gain some degree of awareness over what we have done and over who we are. The self-coaching speaker embraces this process so new realities and realizations can be consciously created out of that.

Develop A Mental Game Plan: Take these three questions as a start in developing your self-coaching action plan.

1. What systems can you develop to increase awareness about yourself? Can you write in a journal? Speak your thoughts into a tape recorder?

2. Who can you partner with to assist you in your self-coaching quest?

3. How will you translate what you learn about yourself into immediately useful action?

❝   ❞

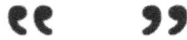

Thoughts About Speaking

The great awareness comes slowly, piece by piece. The path of spiritual growth is a path of lifelong learning. The experience of spiritual power is basically a joyful one.

M. Scott Peck

One of the main focuses of my training sessions is to help individuals find their unique voices in the learning process. We all have our strengths, our weaknesses, our styles of learning, our personalities. Developing introspective sensitivity to these issues is critical to long-term success.

Joshua Waitzkin

We now accept the fact that learning is a lifelong process of keeping abreast of change. And the most pressing task is to teach people how to learn.

Peter Drucker

The Mental Game Of Speaking

Are You A Mentally Tough Speaking Athlete?

Can you play at the top of your game on demand? How do you handle the rigors of the high stress professional speaking game? Mental toughness is the ability to thrive on stress and to perform in the upper ranges of our potential more often. The top athletes who possess mental toughness live this every day. Professional speakers are the pro athletes of the business world. The speakers who continually perform to their potential over a lifetime know what it takes to build and maintain a strong mental game.

Here are some tools and attitudes that you, as a mentally tough speaking athlete, can hold about yourself, your audiences and the speaking business. Reflect on them, discuss them with others and write about them in your journal. Use them to build your mental toughness.

1. **You Don't Hope For An Easy Life. You Strive To Be A Strong Person.** Top athletes seek the rigors of competition and thrive on seeing how they rise to the occasion. You seek challenging opportunities and realize the speaking business is not for the faint of heart. You continually seek assignments which help you grow personally and professionally.

2. **You Love The Craziness Of The Pro Speaking Business.** You accept the often ambiguous and unpredictable nature of our business and learn to adapt, be flexible and overcome the inevitable curves thrown at you. You flow like a mentally tough athlete handling

197

every roadblock imaginable with poise and mastery.

3. **You Have A Mistake Management System.** Athletes make mistakes every time they compete. They have a system to maintain their confidence and refocus on the task at hand immediately. When you make an error, you breathe, relax, smile or joke, recover and maintain poise and balance. You practice "ad-libbed" humorous recovery phrases and have backup plans to handle any problem contingencies in your programs.

4. **You View "Tough Audiences" As Being Your Teachers.** You reframe them as partners in co-creating a valuable learning experience you both share. The more difficult your audience, the greater the victory in winning them over and the more you raise the bar on your influencing skills. Any win is more meaningful when it is more difficult to achieve.

5. **You Use The Specificity Of Training Principle**. You rehearse in your mind and in actuality, using all props, aids, and movements key elements of your program exactly as they will be so there are no surprises. Olympic stars believe that practice does not make perfect...it makes permanent. Only perfect practice makes perfect.

6. **You View "Speaking Slumps" As Opportunities For Growth.** You view these as a normal part of a speaker's development. You examine the "slump" or plateau, learn from it and use it to go to the next level. You are careful as to how you define a slump so you don't create one when one isn't there.

7. **You Use The Concept Of Automaticity.** You over-prepare and know your material cold so your mind is free to do audience calibration. You

read the audience instead of being in your head "remembering" what to do or say next. This allows you to be creatively extemporaneous, and to be in relationship with your audience. You are audience-centered and meet their needs at every moment.

8. **You Use Negative Thinking And Visualization.** You are a positive thinker, yet you also use negativity thinking or mastery visualization where you plan ahead for potential problem contingencies and practice responses to unusual or difficult speaking circumstances. You plan and hope for the best, but you open your eyes to potential bumps in the road in advance.

9. **You Take A Strategic Stance About Difficulties In The Business.** You look back to see how far you've come in the business and how each challenging event toughens you mentally to be able to handle higher levels of stress. You have perspective and can execute tactically as you hold a long-range, wise, strategic viewpoint.

10. **You Use Periodization To Recover From Stress.** Our business is exciting yet energy-draining. You create a periodization scheduling system for allowing your body and mind to heal regularly and to restore energy reserves so you can operate at peak more often. Athletes know they can't train, compete and work continuously. They schedule days off and mini-vacations each day for recovery.

Top athletes and speakers train with dedicated precision, know when and how to recover, take the strategic long-term view and execute to their optimum abilities. Use the mental game secrets of sports stars and take your speaking game to the next level.

❝ ❞

Thoughts About Speaking

Learning how to learn is life's most important skill.

Tony Buzan

It is only when we forget all our learning that we begin to know.

Henry David Thoreau

He who learns but does not think, is lost!
He who thinks but does not learn is in great danger.

Confucius

Want To Give Better Speeches?

Get Into The Peak Performance Zone!

You're giving the best speaking performance of your life. You can't miss. You're red hot. Everything you try is working. You're on a major roll. You're flowing. In the zone. How'd you do that?

We've all been in the zone at one time or another. Many people think getting there is accidental. After all, how often do you get into the zone, maybe 10% of the year? Another 10% of the time you're performing your very worst, no matter what you do, according to the law of averages. That leaves 80% of the time you can actually do something about your performance. This 80% represents how well a person will perform through a year of speaking, and it's all about the mental game. That's where mental toughness and inside knowledge about the psychology of peak performance can help you.

You can prepare to enter the zone, although you cannot will it to happen. In other words, you can set up the mental-emotional-physical conditions that help you get in the proper mind set to perform well, but you can't guarantee the zone will appear. But using your best efforts to enter the zone is far better than either giving up on it, leaving it to chance or accepting that you'll speak poorly on the platform that day. Instead, take charge of your speaking performance by priming your mind.

Here are the phrases athletes, business people, physicians, students, actors, writers, speakers and others have used to describe the zone:

- Tuned In
- Focused
- Right There

- On Autopilot
- Rolling
- Everything Is Clicking
- Switched On
- In The Groove
- Flowing
- Peak Performance
- Zoning
- In Control
- Floating
- Lights Out
- Treeing
- Out Of Your Mind
- In The Tunnel
- In The Cocoon
- On A Roll
- Red Hot

There are countless others. What are the terms you use to describe the zone?

Here is a working definition to get us started in understanding this fascinating phenomenon. Some clinicians and researchers refer to the zone as an Ideal Performance State, or IPS, as the ultimate mind-body connection. This is the internal mental, emotional and physical state required for entry to the zone. This is the mind-body balance that you are attempting to achieve prior to all your speaking experiences.

You are seeking an integrated, harmonious experience where your mind and body are effortlessly working together, in a natural, on-target performance, leaving you feeling that something special has just occurred.

The higher reaches of the zone are characterized by almost flawless execution, a merging with action and feelings of total control, confidence and invincibility.

Here are 34 common zone characteristics I and others have identified. I've made this into a checklist for you to use in coaching sessions, practice sessions and before performances to help you mentally practice getting into the zone, and also as a post-performance tool to see how your mental game behaved while you were on stage. Take this with you to your speaking programs and refer to it often. Assess yourself with it various times a year to see your progress.

1. ☐ Your muscles are relaxed and loose.

2. ☐ You have a calm and quiet mental state with low self talk.

3. ☐ You have low anxiety, an absence of fear, and a feeling that there is no pressure on you to perform.

4. ☐ You have high energy.

5. ☐ You are optimistic and positive.

6. ☐ Your performance is enjoyable.

7. ☐ Your performance is effortless.

8. ☐ Your performance is automatic, instinctive and spontaneous.

9. ☐ Your mind and body are effortlessly working together in harmony.

10. ☐ You experience a sense of powerful momentum.

11. ☐ You have high self-confidence.

12. ☐ You are mentally alert and intense.

13. ☐ You are, and feel like, you are in control, without having to exert conscious control.

14. ☐ You are focused and concentrated.

15. ☐ You have flexible attention.

16. ☐ You are in the cocoon of focus, where your present activity seems to be your whole world.

17. ☐ You ignore internal or external distractions.

18. ☐ You feel unrushed, have plenty of time, and time may seem to actually slow down.

19. ☐ You have extraordinary awareness.

20. ☐ You have on-your-game technical perfection.

21. ☐ You ignore your mistakes or minimize them mentally.

22. ☐ You focus on process, not product.

23. ☐ You have a feeling of physical lightness.

24. ☐ You easily anticipate what is to come.

25. ☐ You have a strong sense of total involvement and immersion with what you are doing.

26. ☐ You have a complete commitment to action.

27. ☐ You feel strong and full of power.

28. ☐ You have a feeling that ordinary, personal limits are being transcended.

29. ☐ You experience a merging of action and awareness, where you do not question, judge or evaluate how you are doing.

30. ☐ You lose your self-consciousness.

31. ☐ You have clear, unambiguous feedback in the moment, without having to stop and reflect.

32. ☐ You have an "autotelic experience", where the activity is justified in and of itself, with no need for external goals, recognition or rewards beyond the experience.

33. ☐ You perceive the universe to be integrated and unified.

34. ☐ You experience the zone as a unique, temporary, almost involuntary experience.

Understand this checklist, use it often and measure all your performances with it. Then learn how to build the mental game tool kit all peak performers have that enable them to access the zone more frequently, and ultimately, almost on command.

Consistently get into the proper mental-emotional-physical space and you'll trigger the zone experience more and more often. The more you know yourself, and what the zone is about, your zone performances will be more frequent, and of a higher quality. Congratulations, you are about to enter the zone.

This checklist is based on the research of Dr. James Loehr, Dr. Charles Garfield, Dr. Kenneth Ravizza, Dr. Mihaly Csikszentmihalyi and Bill Cole, MS, MA.

❝   ❞

Thoughts About Speaking

A good teacher must be able to put himself
in the place of those who find learning hard.

Eliphas Levi

Instead of giving money to found colleges to promote
learning, why don't they pass a constitutional
amendment prohibiting anybody from learning anything?
If it works as good as the Prohibition one did, why, in
five years we would have the smartest race of people on
earth.

Will Rogers

Learning never exhausts the mind.

Leonardo da Vinci

How To Pace Your Speeches

Talk Too Fast Or Too Slow
And You Will Lose Your Audience

Here's How To Avoid That
And Make A Great Impression

What's worse for you, a speaker who drags along, making you wait for every word, or a race horse who you can't keep up with no matter how hard you listen? They are both irritating. They both make being an audience member very difficult. And both styles don't endear themselves to you.

Both types of speakers may not be aware of the pace they use. But both have a very negative effect on their audience. This will help you understand how to use pacing in your presentations and how to avoid the needless errors so may speakers make in this area. Let's look at the reasons for rushing and speaking too ponderously.

Why do you rush our speaking? Four reasons:

1.   Nerves, self-doubt, uncertainty.

2.   Positive excitement of the situation.

3.   Wanting to get all your material in.

4.   Wanting to make the ending time deadline.

You may tend to rush at the beginning of your talk and during Q and A sessions, as these are the most nervous times for most speakers. You often don't even know you are speaking rapidly. But one way to tell is if your voice is rising in pitch and starting to constrict.

1.   Why do you speak too slowly from the platform? Six reasons:

2. You don't know your material and have to retrieve it from memory or notes.

3. You don't know the order of your program and must refer to notes.

4. You are afraid and that locks you up.

5. You are a very careful type of person and don't want to make even one mistake.

6. You think if you speak fast you will lose people.

7. You never speak fast, even in real life.

You may tend to begin to drag in your pacing when thinking of answers to questions, when something unusual happens and you don't know what to do and when covering very technical material that requires great precision.

I don't want to give you the idea that rushing and dragging are both bad and to be eliminated 100% from your speaking. You really don't want to speak in a uniform, constant pace, unless putting the audience to sleep is a major goal. This is a fabulous style if you are a hypnotist doing an induction.

I find the best speakers have a dialogue with their audience. They don't do a data download or hold court, they actually converse and exchange energy with the audience. Talk with your audience. Don't give a speech.

The best speakers vary their pace, all the way through their speech to keep everyone on their toes. Here's how and when to vary your speaking pace:

Slow down:

1. When you want to make a special point.

2. After a particularly fast period of speaking to let the audience catch their breath.

3.   When you want the audience to think more.

4.   After you ask rhetorical questions.

5.   For dramatic pauses.

6.   To display emotion.

You can create white space, or quiet pauses to let the audience catch up to you or to reflect. The faster you speak, the more pauses you should have so the audience can stay with you. Let them digest your material. Don't speak so fast, so often that the audience feels like it is drinking from a fire hose.

A good rule is to pause slightly after a sentence, pause longer after a paragraph, and pause longest after a module. Help your audience grasp your content by organizing it for them using verbal white space, just as a book editor does when they use book design principles. Pausing also gives you time to gather yourself.

Speed up:

1.   When you sense you are losing the audience.

2.   When you want to create excitement and raise the energy in the room.

3.   When you are telling a story and want to be dramatic.

4.   After a particularly slow period of speaking.

Now you are probably much more aware of your speaking tendencies when it comes to pacing. Continue to notice what you do. Vary what you do. Use pacing with good intention and your audiences will thank you by being attentive every step of the way through your speech. Good luck.

"   "

Thoughts About Speaking

Change is the end result of all true learning.

Leo Buscaglia

The noblest pleasure is the joy of understanding.

Leonardo da Vinci

Education is learning what you didn't even know you
didn't know.

Daniel J. Boorstin

WRITING AND USING HUMOR

How NOT To Use Humor In A Speech

Avoid These 46 Gaffes Speakers Make When Using Humor

There is an apocryphal story about a young speaker asking an old platform pro about the value of humor in professional speaking. The youngster said, "Should I have humor in my speeches?" To which the old pro stated, "Only if you want to get paid". The moral of the story? You won't go far in professional speaking without some humor in your programs.

I speak professionally and write humor for myself and other speakers. I have huge files of all types of humor on many topics, and use those as a basis for customizing humor for each audience. How do you see this next joke fitting in a speech? One time a woman was talking to the speaker right before his program. She asked, "Do you get very nervous before a speech?" "Not at all", he says. She then asked, "So what are you doing in the ladies restroom?" This could be used for many topics: stress, speaking, hurrying, absent-mindedness, pre-program preparation and self-awareness, among others.

A speaker told this next story at a parent conference. A teen-aged girl was going out to a party one night. As she was about to leave her mother said, "Have a nice time tonight Dear". The girl yelled back, "Don't tell me what to do!" This was a big hit, because everyone in the audience had either been a teenager once or now had teens as children. They could relate to the story as being true. This joke was an excellent fit because it matched the audience, matched the theme of the conference, it was clean, easy to tell and the speaker could use it as an entree for further discussion.

You see now how speakers can use humorous stories, but sometimes an attempt at humor goes down the wrong path.

One time I was in the audience when a well-known speaker began what was to be a funny story, and by the time he delivered the punch line, the audience was so lost, the auditorium was dead silent. The humor bombed and the speaker was devastated. It was his best humorous story. His signature story. But it fell flatter than a day-old pancake at a family reunion.

What did he do wrong? He left out a critical piece of information that got the audience lost. He used a "big ten dollar word" that left the audience confused. He started to chuckle to himself mid way through, distracting the audience. And he botched the punch line by rushing and mispronouncing a critical word. Other than that, he told the story fine.

That brings us to our main purpose. Do you use humor in your speeches? How comfortable are you in telling jokes and using humorous stories? Do you use other humor devices in your programs? How do your audiences respond to your attempts at humor? If you need some humor help, I'll show you the way to creating more humorous speaking programs, and reaping the many benefits that come from being a funny speaker.

Humor is perhaps considered the hardest art form there is. When an actor does a poor job, the audience can sit there and simply not respond or they possibly may respect his effort with some light applause. When a musician does poorly, they usually still receive polite applause. When a comedian fails in his craft, there is either dead silence, or worse, catcalls and boos. Challenges and insults. The audience feels cheated. Comics call it dying on stage. The comic is supposed to make people actually laugh, not mildly entertain them or worse, use people's time. When the comedian succeeds, we say "He killed the audience". Sounds like warfare. In some ways it is. In the humor game, the mandate is clear. The audience MUST laugh, or you have failed. That's a pretty high standard to achieve consistently.

Humor can be considered a scary art form for speakers. It's not for the faint of heart, nor for the ill-prepared. You have to know what you are doing, be well-rehearsed and be confident in executing a funny bit. Show weakness and lack of confidence and the audience will eat you alive. Getting consistent laughs from humorous stories, jokes and other humor devices is not an impossibility. You can be funny if you know the basic laws of humor, what makes something funny, what makes something UN-funny, and how to deliver a humorous bit. An excellent starting point is to know and understand the many ways a humorous piece can fail, so you can avoid these needless gaffes.

I'm sure you've seen speakers who have ruined a funny story or joke, or who just can't seem to pull off any type of humor. As a public speaking skills coach, I've extensively studied the failings of speakers when it comes to humor. For your benefit, I've compiled a list of 46 different ways speakers can botch up a humorous story, joke or other funny bit. Know these, and your chances of avoiding them and actually being funny will skyrocket!

1. Telling shaggy-dog stories (terminally long stories with a weak punch line).

2. Having only one punch line in a long story.

3. Telling only jokes and no stories.

4. Thinking you have to be as funny as a standup comic.

5. Telling jokes unrelated to a point or your speech theme.

6. Thinking puns and other filler humor will get big laughs.

7. Rushing the story.

8. Rushing/mangling/muffling the punch line.

9. Incongruous body language.

10. Low LPM (Laughs Per Minute).

11. Adding unnecessary details in the story.

12. Using words and phrases your audience doesn't understand.

13. Forgetting any portions of the joke.

14. Making the joke up as you go.

15. Not rehearsing the joke.

16. Trying a new version of the joke for the first time.

17. Unclear lead-up to the punch line so the audience gets lost.

18. Letting the punch line slip out in advance, instead of saving it for the end.

19. Making the punch line so obvious, anyone can see it coming a mile away.

20. Pausing mid-joke and losing momentum.

21. Using voices and accents you can't carry well.

22. Laughing at the joke as you tell it.

23. Making side comments or being parenthetical mid-joke.

24. Asking rhetorical questions and expecting the audience not to respond.

25. Back-tracking during the joke.

26. Not placing the punch line last or near the very end.

27. Reciting a joke from memory with no inflection.

28. Telling a joke that is better suited and funnier when being read.

29. Stepping on the punch line laugh. This refers to the joke teller continuing to speak right after the punch line, thereby ruining the ability of the audience to laugh, since they need to stop to listen to what else the humorist has to say.

30. Poor punch line timing.

31. Not matching the humor to the audience's age, mood, expertise, language, culture and religion.

32. Using material that makes the audience uncomfortable.

33. Asking permission to tell the joke instead of making it sound natural.

34. Saying "Stop me if you've heard this one".

35. Giving away the joke by saying, "Didja hear the one about the three elephants?"

36. Announcing, "Here comes a joke", or "This is a funny joke" or "I hope you like this joke".

37. Repeating or explaining a joke for those who did not think it was funny.

38. Stopping mid-joke and starting a new one if you think the first one is not working.

39. Asking, "Didja get it? "Funny, huh?"

40. Putting down anyone who does not get your joke.

41. Getting angry or flustered that people did not laugh at your joke.

42. Allowing someone else to butt in or finish your joke.

43. Asking for help if you forget the joke.

44. Immediately launching another joke if the first one falls flat.

45. Bombarding your audience by telling too many jokes in a row.

46. Making fun of a weaker group of people, or of people who can't defend themselves.

I hope this encourages you to use more humor after reading this list of humor no-no's. Usually speakers comment, "I never knew there was so much to comedy". Being humorous is VERY possible, even for those who don't think they are naturally funny.

If you work at it, and become a student of comedy, you will make great strides. I truly encourage you to add humor to your speaking programs. It will enhance your material, your reputation, and, your bottom line.

" "

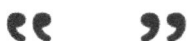

Thoughts About Speaking

A good teacher can inspire hope, ignite the imagination,
and instill a love of learning.

Brad Henry

Tell me and I forget. Teach me and I remember.
Involve me and I learn.

Benjamin Franklin

Talking and eloquence are not the same: to speak,
and to speak well, are two things.

Ben Jonson

Tell A Joke On Yourself
When You Speak

When I was hired as the presentation coach for a west-coast politician I was asked to write some humor he could use in his stump speeches.

Because he possessed such a huge resume, and he was known as a very wealthy individual, I had to create some material that would reduce the natural resistance his audiences would have for him.

Why would they have an aversion to him naturally, and think he was an ego-maniac, before they even heard him open his mouth?

That's because people axiomatically believe wealthy people got that way by stepping on someone else. And that someone with such an impressive history must think they are a big deal. That they are BETTER than the audience. Pompous.

This is called audience resistance. The audience has this mind set before the speech even begins, and your job as the speaker is to reduce or eliminate it. If you don't, you will never build rapport and trust with your audiences. You need that bond to be persuasive and get them to listen, and hopefully, to act on what you are saying. Otherwise, what's the point?

How do you reduce resistance? Take a shot at yourself before someone else does. Show that you are just a regular person, not someone special. Puncture your own balloon.

The best way to do this is to use self-deprecating humor. That's where you direct the joke at yourself. Make yourself the target and see the audience laugh at you. They then know that you don't take yourself so seriously, and that you can laugh at yourself, and THEY will relax and begin to like you.

Here are a few jokes that swirl around in the political ether that we used to very good effect.

Americans don't like sending politicians to Washington, but unfortunately that's as far away as we can send them.

Or how about this one that describes how we feel about the value of politicians.

A man flying in a hot air balloon realizes he is lost. He reduces his altitude and spots a man in a field down below. He lowers the balloon further and shouts, "Excuse me, can you tell me where I am?"

The man below says, "Yes, you're in a hot air balloon, about 30 feet above this field."

"You must be an engineer," says the balloonist.

"I am. How did you know?"

"Everything you told me is technically correct, but it's of no use to anyone."

The man below says, "You must be a politician."

"I am. But how did you know?"

"You don't know where you are, or where you're going, but you expect me to be able to help. You're in the same position you were before we met, but now it's my fault."

And this one.

My daughter told me a cute joke yesterday.

Q: Why did God create politicians?

A: In order to make used car salesmen look good.

Tell a few jokes on yourself early in your speeches and watch your audiences begin to relax, lighten up and start to see you as being just like them, an ordinary human being.

Then move ahead to deliver an enthusiastic and inspiring speech.

❝ ❞
Thoughts About Speaking

Efforts to develop critical thinking falter in practice
because too many professors still lecture to passive
audiences instead of challenging students to apply
what they have learned to new questions.

Derek Bok

When I give a lecture, I accept that people look at their
watches, but what I do not tolerate is when they look at
it and raise it to their ear to find out if it stopped.

Marcel Achard

Within the confines of the lecture hall, no other
virtue exists but plain intellectual integrity.

Max Weber

How To Customize Humor For Speaking

There are millions of jokes out there. Most of them use well-known formulas as their basis. You can utilize these formulas to re-write them for your customized purposes. You will then look like a genius, and have "original" humor targeted to your specific audience. Here's how to do that.

The Original Joke

The psychology instructor had just finished a lecture on mental health and was giving an oral test.

Speaking specifically about manic depression, she asked, "How would you diagnose a patient who walks back and forth screaming at the top of his lungs one minute, then sits in a chair weeping uncontrollably the next?"

A young man in the rear raised his hand and answered, "A basketball coach?"

Ways To Customize The Joke

Change the subjects:

Change she to he.

Change she to a boss.

Change she to Dr. Phil.

Change she to _____.

Change young man to _____.

Change the punch line:

Change basketball coach to a boss.

Change basketball coach to an admin.

Change basketball coach to an executive.

Change basketball coach to the CEO.

Change basketball coach to an engineer.

Change basketball coach to a _____.

The Original Joke

A young woman took her troubles to a psychiatrist. "Doctor, you must help me," she pleaded. "It's gotten so that every time I date a nice guy, I end up in bed with him. And then afterward, I feel guilty and depressed for a week."

"I see," nodded the psychiatrist. "And you, no doubt, want me to strengthen your will power and resolve in this matter."

"For God's sake, NO!" exclaimed the woman. "I want you to fix it so I won't feel guilty and depressed afterward."

Ways To Customize The Joke

Change the subject and topic:

Change young woman to _____.

Change to anyone you will be speaking to.

Change to anyone your audience would like to see you make fun of.

Change topic to_____.

Over eating

Drinking too much.

Lack of exercise.

Smoking.

Workaholics.

Slackers.

Coffee drinkers.

It's dangerous to use stock jokes gathered from joke books, and from the internet, and tell them as is. If you read them there, so have other people. The best humor is original, but you can create near-original humor if you recognize joke formulas and re-craft them for your purposes. Collect jokes but look for the formulas in them. Then you can create a nice stable of jokes of your own. More importantly, you can craft original, targeted humor for any audience you will face.

❝   ❞

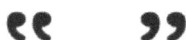

Thoughts About Speaking

I love my lecture tours. I get up onstage. I have my
stack of books and a glass of water and a microphone.
No podium, no distance between me and the audience,
and I just talk to people and get all excited and tell a lot
of jokes, and sing some songs, and read from my work
and remind people how powerful they are and how
beautiful they are.

Suzan-Lori Parks

Every idea is an incitement...
eloquence may set fire to reason.

Oliver Wendell Holmes, Jr.

Talking and eloquence are not the same:
to speak and to speak well are two things.
A fool may talk, but a wise man speaks.

Heinrich Heine

Speaking Performance Tips

We Can Learn From Johnny Carson Speech Coaching From The King Of Late-Night TV

A friend of mine passed away today. A living legend in show business. Johnny Carson. Well, he wasn't exactly a true friend of mine, because I never had the pleasure of meeting Johnny, but I still felt I knew him as well as any friend. He graced our living rooms and bedrooms each night for 34 years. His show was a cultural marvel and icon. He was a show biz treasure.

Stars and celebrities have come out today, lamenting his passing and giving testament to his greatness as a person, and as a performer. Jay Leno said, "No single individual has had as great an impact on television as Johnny. He was the gold standard".

I learned much from Johnny the performer. He started his show biz life as a magician, ventriloquist and announcer. He was a funnyman from the outset of his career. He hosted radio and TV shows and emceed awards shows. If you saw Johnny in action, what do you remember about him? What did he teach you about being a performer? I'd like to share some of the many things Johnny taught me about performing and being in front of people. He's helped me tremendously in my speaking career. I hope he can help you too.

(Bonus Question: In his first show in 1962, who was his first guest? Answer at the end)

What Speakers Can Learn From Johnny Carson

1. **Trademarks.** The whole TV show was one big brand. Ed McMahon's "Heeeeere's Johnny!". The Tonight show musical theme. Johnny with his signature golf swing to end the monologue. Johnny's nervous mannerisms and phrases. The

sketch characters. Doc Severinsen with his colorfully outrageous outfits. What can you do to create memorable, signature brands that your audiences will love?

2. **Great Listener.** Many talk show hosts just did not listen well. David Brenner recounts how the typical TV host, after David would try a set-up line like, "I just bought a parrot today" (hoping for a straight line of Oh, really? to crack a joke) would switch gears off topic and say something like, "You're from Philly, right?", and ruin the joke. Johnny would always pick up that there was a joke coming and accommodate it with the perfect set-up line. He would be the ultimate reaction host to his guests. How well do you listen to your audience during your talk?

3. **Thinking Funny.** Johnny was a master magician, stand-up comic and radio and TV show host, and one of his best attributes, says second banana Ed McMahon, Johnny's sidekick for over 30 years, was his ability to simply BE funny, act funny and react funny. Often, Ed never knew what Johnny would actually do, but he knew it would stem from Johnny's uncanny knack at thinking funny and seeing the comical in everything. How can you think and be funny in your speeches?

4. **Audience Rapport.** Johnny was known as a kind, caring, giving person, not an ego-maniac, even though he was a big star. He was appreciative of his success, often saying, "Anyone is expendable". There was nothing phony or stuck-up about him, and people felt like they really, genuinely knew him. He made everyone comfortable in spite of his well-known shyness in large groups, paradoxical to his comfort in front of the camera. How well do you create rapport with your audiences?

5. **Modesty.** Even with Johnny's great fame, fortune and celebrity status, the average viewer felt they knew Johnny as a friend. Somehow Johnny was able to transmit this intimacy through the television tube each night and come across like a long-time buddy. Johnny never bragged or posed as a star, or made anyone feel beneath him, and how many people in show business are known simply by their first name? In spite of his huge fame, he had a true humbleness and humanity about him. How do your audiences see you, on and off the platform? Do you have congruence and credibility?

6. **Selfless.** Johnny played off of his guests, and even though it was his show, he never upstaged anyone. He never took himself seriously. He knew how to get out of the way and let the stars shine. In fact, countless stars still tell of how he "rescued" them during moments they were bombing, something for which they are eternally grateful. How can you involve your audiences and make them the stars of your program?

7. **Consistent Professionalism.** Johnny Carson parted the curtains and walked out on that Tonight Show stage over 5,000 times in his 34-year career. For many years he did five 90-minute shows per week, always staying fresh, original and topical. He won four consecutive Emmy Awards, and a Presidential Medal of Freedom, among other awards. In 1993, he was celebrated by the prestigious Kennedy Center Honors for career achievement. How do you stay fresh and original? How do you maintain high levels of professionalism each time you speak?

8. **Scripted And Unscripted.** The Tonight Show was tightly-written and well-rehearsed, but there were moments of wildly hysterical spontaneous mad-cap humor antics. Johnny was a witty, alert, observant performer who could seize the audience by the humor lapels and yank

them hither and yon. He was a master ad-libber and could react and run with anything his guests (both human and animal) presented him. How scripted are you? How well do you ad-lib and go with the flow?

9. **Winning Formula.** It is no accident that anytime you tune into any TV talk show, the familiar band, monologue, desk and chairs, parade of guests and skits are ever present. Why? Producers and writers have learned that you don't change a winning game, and you have to give audiences what they like and want. What is your winning formula for your speeches?

10. **Entertainment Value.** With his boyish, puckish charm, good-natured, gentile manners and his down-home style, Johnny exuded a contagious enjoyment of his guests. When he reared back in his chair convulsed in laughter, we could not help but laugh with him. Johnny knew how to get the laugh, play for the applause, milk the situation and be the ever-aware performer, no matter the happening. How much entertainment value do your programs have? How do you best entertain your audiences?

Johnny Carson was the last voice America heard before they drifted off to sleep each night. We will miss Johnny for the charming ways he entertained us all those years. I hope you enjoyed this tribute to one of my all-time idols, and I hope you learned how to be a better speaker from one of the legends of show business.

Bonus question Answer: His very first guest in 1962 was Groucho Marx.

❝ ❞

Thoughts About Speaking

Enthusiasm is the greatest asset you can possess, for it can take you further than money, power or influence.

Dada Vaswani

Power is a tool, influence is a skill; one is a fist, the other a fingertip.

Nancy Gibbs

Well-timed silence hath more eloquence than speech.

Martin Farquhar Tupper

QUESTION AND ANSWER SESSIONS

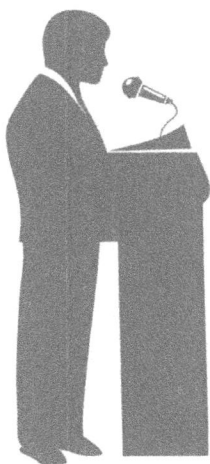

Ten Tips For Handling Questions-And-Answers

Prepare For The Toughest Questions You Will Ever Face

Most speakers, even experienced ones, often dread taking questions from the audience. After all, the speaker has less control when the audience gets involved like this, and no one really knows what to expect. But many experienced speakers come to enjoy the question and answer (Q and A) period because they know they may learn something new, and this gives the audience their best chance to customize the talk by asking specific questions and in going deeper into the material.

I hope you begin to see the Q and A session as a valuable moment in your speech, one where you and the audience can truly be in dialogue and create a deeper intimacy. Here are my top ten tips to help you improve this critical time in any talk.

1. **Face The Questioner, And Stop All Movement And Speaking.** Show respect and be classy by looking exclusively at the person asking the question. The audience should then follow your cue.

2. **Repeat The Question, No Matter What.** Perhaps the top pet peeve of audiences the world over is not being able to hear the question. The speaker and people near the questioner can hear, but often no one else has a clue as to what was said. Repeating the question--always--is one mark of a speaking pro.

3. **Begin Answering The Question To The Asker And Then Spread Out To The Aud-**

ience At Large. It shows respect to begin having a conversation one on one and then broaden it to everyone else.

4. **Ask The Person To Repeat The Question If Necessary.** Maybe you or the audience did not hear the question well, or you want more time to think. There's no harm in asking for it again.

5. **Seek Understanding By Restating The Question To The Person.** If you need even more time, or you want to make sure you and everyone else truly "gets" the question, rephrase it in your own words, maintaining the essence of the original question.

6. **Pause Before Answering.** Take just a moment for the question to sink in for the audience. Waiting also makes you look more in control.

7. **Speak Directly To The Question.** Aim at least part of your answer at the question. After that, it would be fine to divert and say other things you want to get in.

8. **Shorter Answers Are Better Than Longer Answers.** Longer answers can bore people, and can make you look defensive. The shorter your answers (make sure they are complete, but not overdone), the more questions can be asked, and this keeps the audience happy.

9. **Turn And Move On To The Next Question.** Once done answering, simply turn to the next question, unless the person has a follow up.

10. **At the End Of The Q And A Period, Move Into Your Concluding Remarks.** Inexperienced speakers often stop their program after the Q and A by saying, "Well, if there are no more questions, I guess that's it." Instead, you want to conclude the Q and A and imme-

diately move into your final summary or wrap up. This looks VERY professional.

Bonus tip: NEVER say "good question" before answering. This is amateurish and annoys people after the first few times the audience hears it. Plus, if you forget to say that, does that mean the question was NOT a good one? You get the point.

Q and A periods don't have to be intimidating if you prepare well, have a strategy for them and practice for them. Audiences love Q and A, and once you become more comfortable in it, you may actually look forward to questions coming your way. It will mark you as an experienced, comfortable, bold speaker.

❝   ❞
Thoughts About Speaking

The key to successful leadership today is influence,
not authority.

Ken Blanchard

Leadership is not about a title or a designation. It's
about impact, influence and inspiration. Impact involves
getting results, influence is about spreading the passion
you have for your work, and you have to inspire
teammates and customers.

Robin S. Sharma

Leadership is influence.

John C. Maxwell

Avoid These 38 Question-And-Answer Mistakes Speakers Make

Whether you're giving a presentation to one person, a small group, or a large gathering, how you handle questions can make you or break you. Your management of questions and answers is a sharp measure of your leadership, and your ability to facilitate a group. Knowing how to handle questions marks you as an expert speaker. You want to be influential and persuasive, and how you deal with Q and A can either build audience rapport, and bring you what you want, or send you packing.

Take at look at these 38 common mistakes presenters make with Q and A. How many of these errors do you commit? How many do you see other speakers commit?

An inexperienced speaker:

1. Allows the questioner to go on at length without helping them organize their question.

2. Fails to restate the question in clear terms.

3. Restates the question word for word, instead of getting its essence.

4. Begins answering while the questioner is still speaking.

5. Appears to not give the questioner respect or take them seriously.

6. Gives an answer only to the questioner, or only to the audience, not both.

7. Says "No comment", "The question is irrelevant", or the like, instead of dealing with it.

8. Gives a great answer, but not to that question.

9. Answers before thinking.

10. Says "Excellent question, or Good question" each time.

11. Uses formulaic techniques, such as, "Can you repeat the question?, in almost every instance.

12. Gives answers that are too long or too short.

13. Stays with one or two questioners and does not encourage questions from the entire room.

14. Becomes defensive in the face of tough questions.

15. Increases resistance in the room by being tense, combative or evasive.

16. Fails to anticipate questions by covering them in the speech content.

17. Does not have answers prepared and practiced in advance.

18. Fails to announce a protocol for the Q and A procedure.

19. Repeats the inflammatory or negative parts of a question.

20. Takes attacks personally, and responds personally.

21. Fails to grasp the core, or real intent behind questions.

22. Fails to make eye contact with the questioner.

23. Is less than truthful, or gives the appearance of evasive hedging.

24. Loses their temper, or appears less than mentally tough.

25. Places hands on hips, crosses arms, and uses other negative body language.

26. Lacks tact and diplomacy.

27. Fails to admit to a mistake or inconsistency.

28. Walks aggressively towards the questioner, or points at them.

29. Allows the Q and A session to drag, become too technical, too arcane or to become boring.

30. Fails to break longer, multipart questions into pieces.

31. Loses control of the room and allows the audience members to take over.

32. Answers specific, narrow questions that the majority of the audience does not care about, rather than answering them after the talk.

33. Fails to reformulate, clarify, or defer irrelevant questions.

34. Fails to anticipate entrapping questions that are being used to set up an attack.

35. Fails to say "I don't know", if they really don't know.

36. Answers in an aggressive, sarcastic or other negative manner that discourages any further questions.

37. Fails to correct inaccurate, misleading or mistaken material.

38. Ends the program by saying, "Well, if there are no more questions, I guess that's it"., instead of delivering prepared, concluding remarks.

Any of these speaking gaffes can cause a loss of your platform credibility. Know the rules of handling Q and A, and you'll appear savvy when you present. Your presentations will be smoother, and your audience will respect you more. Leading expert, spirited discussions around Q and A, you'll sell them on yourself and your ideas far better.

"   "

Thoughts About Speaking

You don't need a big close, as many sales reps believe.
You risk losing your customer when you save all the
good stuff for the end. Keep the customer actively
involved throughout your presentation,
and watch your results improve.

Harvey Mackay

When you really need help, people will respond.
Sincerity means dropping the image facade and showing
a willingness to be vulnerable. Tell it the way it is, lumps
and all. Don't worry if your presentation isn't perfect;
ask from your heart. Keep it simple,
and people will open up to you.

Jack Canfield

There are good leaders who actively guide and bad
leaders who actively misguide. Hence, leadership is
about persuasion, presentation and people skills.

Shiv Khera

How To Handle Hostile Questions

A few years ago I was hired by a politician to be his Head Speech Writer and presentation coach. I worked with him across three campaigns. He ran for State Assembly, State Insurance Commissioner and Governor. These are some of the strategies I gave him those years to help him handle tough questions on stage, on TV and on radio.

You can use these strategies also for your own speaking.

Use These Tactics To Set The Stage In Your Favor

1. Your assistant and introducer sets the protocol for the meeting before it begins. "Tonight, Mr. So and So will be speaking for 15 minutes or so and then he will take questions. Please make your question short and to the point so we can get to as many people as possible in the time allowed. We regret that we won't have time for follow up questions, but he will remain after to chat with you". After that, YOU need to clearly be the leader, the one in charge of the floor.

2. You reinforce repeatedly that you want more questions, not long deep ones. "We want to hear from as many people as possible tonight".

3. STOP SHORT anyone asking a follow up question, refer to the above protocol.

4. Share the wealth on getting to more people.

5. Stay away from drilling down into an answer.

6. Refer them to your white papers, book and web site.

Be A Diplomatic, Yet Forceful Leader From The Platform

1. YOU must show leadership from the platform and control the audience. No one else can do that for you.

2. You are NOT REQUIRED to answer the person's question at all. You can completely IGNORE IT and give your own response.

3. DO NOT endlessly defend yourself or your positions. You do NOT want to be in their control by answering to them.

4. The higher the degree of attack, the less I would answer the question. I would turn it back on your opponent and make him answer YOUR questions.

5. DISMISS their attacking questions with the back of your verbal hand and move on to what YOU want to say.

6. The person who asks the best questions controls the debate. Ask THEM to answer some of YOUR charges as to why your opponent has not done this or that, or why he still does this or that.

7. You can ignore any portions of a person's questions, if they ask multiple questions. Just respond the way YOU want to.

8. Be adept at quickly, yet respectfully cutting a questioner off so they don't ramble and dominate. Do NOT allow someone to ramble on.

9. Be diplomatic by reframing the question into favorable terms for you.

10. NEVER repeat negative or emotionally charged words the questioner uses.

Be Strategic

1. Have at least three of your people (staff/supporters) ready with "positive hip pocket questions" to ask IMMEDIATELY after a negative question has been asked. You will call on that person and avoid a string of negative questions to gain traction and harm the speech tone.

2. Smile and remain calm. Stay centered, like you are doing martial arts.

3. Use your quick wit and sense of humor to deflate the pointed animosity of the negative questioner.

4. Take your time before answering. Good time to take a drink. Have water nearby.

5. Summarize their question and position it the way YOU want to answer it. This shows you were listening and reduces some of the questioner's resistance, that they were at least heard fully by you. It also demonstrates great respect for everyone in the room and marks you as the leader you are.

Ten Pointed Counter Phrases To Use Against Hostile Questioners

You can use any of these after a your opponent attacks you with a comment thrown out from the audience, or from a direct question attack:

1. Mr. So and So, don't the people in this district deserve an ethically-run campaign?

"The people of this state DESERVE BETTER than what my opponent has to offer when he says..."

Bill Cole, MS MA

2. "I was hoping to debate my opponent HIMSELF on that VERY ISSUE, but he seems to be avoiding me all these months".

3. "I know you are unhappy with my view on that, but the VAST MAJORITY of people in this state/district agree that..."

4. "I'll tell you what is REALLY UPSETTING to the people in this district."...and then attack what your opponent has done/not done.

5. They attack you on a mailed "hit piece": Mr. So and So, will you apologize for your shameful hit piece and dirty political mailer?

"My opponent should apologize to the people of this district for his shameful stand on x and his highly inappropriate behavior regarding the xx. What he has done is WRONG and frankly, IRRESPONSIBLE".

6. If they attack you on your "misleading and non-factual flyer"-- Mr. So and So, do you think that is appropriate and fair?

"What is highly inappropriate and insulting to the people of this district is my opponent's attitude about BBB when he..."

7. Do you feel you should apologize to your opponent for your hate speech against him?

"I think my opponent is perfectly capable of defending himself. Again, I have been waiting almost five months for him to answer my call for another public debate."

8. Mr. So and So, you really should pledge now to stop using these sleazy campaign tactics. Will you do that right now, in public?

"I think that is an admission that you've lost this argument Sir."

9. They attack you viciously.

"THANK YOU FOR YOUR CANDOR in criticizing my position. I'LL TAKE THAT AS AN INVITATION TO BE EQUALLY CANDID about my views of how my opponent is harming the people of this district."

10. Mr. So and So, isn't it the right and proper thing to do to stop your slanderous hit propaganda?

"I'll tell you what is right and proper. That's for my opponent to stop HIS xxxx and his yyyy and to step up and debate me on the issues, in public, instead of behind my back."

How Might You Handle Tough Questions

1. Brush them off and move on.

2. Answer shortly and redirect to your talking points.

3. Do NOT give too much detail.

4. You do NOT need to answer every one of their points.

5. Do not appear defensive. Remain calm and open looking in your posture.

6. Do not allow them to make follow-up questions and dominate.

7. Do NOT allow them to make ad hominem attacks on you or your staff.

8. Never speculate about anything.

What Are Some Common Concerns About Hostile Questions?

1. Things may get out of control.

2. They may ask something you can't answer.

3. Something embarrassing may come up.

4. You may be caught in a lie or contradiction.

5. You may be ganged up on by more than one person.

6. There may be too many negative questions compared to supportive ones.

7. You might lose personal control and get angry.

8. You might look nervous.

You can see that politics is known as a blood sport. It's not for the faint of heart. You may never dabble in politics, but we can all learn how the masterful politicians handle themselves on stage.

🙶 🙷

Thoughts About Speaking

PowerPoint may not be of any use for you in a
presentation, but it may liberate you in another way,
an artistic way. Who knows.

David Byrne

Presentation skills are key. People who work for you
represent your brand. You want them to present
themselves - and represent you - in a certain way.

Marc Benioff

Pop is a little bit theatrical. That's the whole vibe. That's
the point - is that it's great music, great melodies, great
hooks. But, on top of it, it's a presentation. There's a
showmanship about it. And that's why I wanted to be
a pop star.

Adam Lambert

SPEAKING TO SPECIAL AUDIENCES

" "

Thoughts About Speaking

The moment that changed me forever was when I had my first seminar with my history professor at the University of Sussex. I realized that history would answer all the questions I had spent my life asking. It was an extraordinary moment.

Philippa Gregory

I write, I teach, I direct. I sail around the world for Holland America two months out of every year doing a seminar where we discuss film or theater and do improvisations.

Troy Donahue

If I go to a seminar and someone like you or someone like him is talking, I'm never part of the group that rushes him directly afterward. I always wait in the back corner with my head down until everyone is gone, and then I go up and do my thing.

Arthur Godfrey

Stop Boring The Board Room

Speaking To "C-Level" Executives

One time not too many years ago my business partner and I were in the boardroom of a major corporation in Silicon Valley, launching a proposal for a very large training contract. Siemens Corporation to be exact. A real player internationally. My partner was beginning our 45-minute PowerPoint presentation to the executive panel convened in front of us. They found our business model fascinating and wanted to know more.

My partner definitely told them more about us. Too much. They were squirming, asking questions "out of order", hurrying him up, and generally looking exasperated at his ponderous, careful, ex-engineer speaking style. Even my not too subtle hints to my partner to speed things up went un-noticed.

Finally, when I took over the presentation, the damage had been done, and in spite of my efforts at enlivening our dog and pony show, the executives had heard enough, and wanted to run out of the board room, screaming all the way.

Don't let this nightmare scenario happen to you. It's easily prevented with some advance reconnaissance and planning on your part. The bottom line? Speaking to executives is different. They are NOT your typical audience. These are the "big dogs".

First, let's examine what executives dislike in a presentation.

What Doesn't Work With Executives

1. Long detailed presentations.

2. Taking questions at the end.

3. PowerPoint in linear order.

4. The bottom line at the end as a summary.

5. Expecting them to sit and listen quietly, endlessly.

6. Taking your time, at a leisurely pace.

7. You talking, with them listening all the way through.

In short, executives are busy. They like to be in charge. Asking questions makes them feel like they are in charge. Being passive is not in their blood. They want to be in the know early. They want the 30,000 foot view before they dig down into the trenches to get the details.

Conference Presentations

Giving a corporate speech at a convention is not the same as giving a presentation to corporate folks on their turf. At a convention the speaker is an invited guest, often paid to speak. The speaker controls 95% or more of the talk, from start to finish. The presentation can simply be a "speech", with little or no interaction with the audience and the audience is generally polite, or at least quietly tolerant. The audience usually does not interrupt, or change agendas. In short, giving a speech to a corporate audience at a meeting is often a controllable, predictable, orderly event.

Corporate Presentations

How about when you make a presentation to a corporate group on their turf? Things are starkly different. The stakes are often very high. Something either very good or potentially very bad may result from your presentation. The pressure can be intimidating. The faces in the audience may not be very supportive or friendly.

Here are five big-picture strategies to help you manage the care and feeding of executives in your next in-house presentation.

What Executives Expect In A Corporate Presentation

1. The executive summary first.

2. Detailed explanations second.

3. Being able to ask questions anytime they want.

4. Exact answers to their questions and concerns.

5. A fluid, flexible presentation style adapted to their needs.

6. I wish I knew those strategies all those years ago in that Siemens boardroom. Here are more now.

The Big Dog Audience

Let's take a look at the characteristics of the "C-level" audience, on their turf.

1. Bottom line-oriented.

2. In a hurry, and impatient.

3. Type-A, high-pressure types.

259

4. Big egos competing for airtime, trying to command the room.

5. Don't suffer fools easily.

6. Think nothing of interrupting the speaker.

7. Q and A can happen at any moment-even at the outset.

8. Ask hard-hitting questions.

9. Not above purposely stressing and embarrassing a speaker to test their mettle.

10. Expect the speaker's conclusion at the beginning.

11. No tolerance for fluff and non-targeted data and content.

12. Don't want stories without a purpose, and won't tolerate long stories.

13. Do not want personal disclosure from a speaker.

14. Expect content tied to their success.

15. Will tell you where you stand as a speaker, and may not be polite about it.

16. They control the presentation clock, and may cut the speaker off, or make them stay longer.

17. Intolerant of minutiae, unless they ask for it.

18. Do not want long PowerPoint presentations.

19. Prefer to be given the bottom line verbally at the outset, with handouts later.

20. Will not tolerate canned presentations.

21. Will not allow speakers to "give a speech".

Corporate Presentations Are "Framed Discussions"

On their turf, you are NOT giving a speech. You are facilitating a dialogue. This conversation is between everyone in the room-the speaker, and all the participants. To succeed in this environment, here is what you need:

1. You must be able to think on your feet-clearly and quickly.

2. You must be able to operate in a quasi-leadership role in a room full of take-charge types.

3. Interactive speaking skills are a must.

4. You must have solid process skills, and be able to assess what they want, and make changes to your presentation on the fly.

5. You must be able to change content and style directions on a moment's notice.

6. You have to withstand the stress that will be flying around in the room.

7. You need to understand group dynamics to assess what is unfolding before your eyes.

8. You will be faced with sometimes unruly, negative, disrespectful behavior that you have no power to control.

9. The presentation is about them, not you as the speaker. You are not a star, or the main event. They are what is important.

10. You must understand how corporate politics works and be attuned to that in your presentation.

11. Have "hip-pocket slides" in reserve. These are the modules or slides you hold back in case you either have extra time to fill, or receive questions on that topic. It makes you look like the real pro that you are.

12. Don't use big words in an effort to impress the "smart executives". Simple is best.

13. Be brisk and respect their time. They are busy people. To them time is money.

14. Don't get locked into a linear PowerPoint or slide presentation that will handcuff you once they begin asking questions out of order.

15. Less is more. Don't complicate the message with fluff or too much detail. Executives want the bottom line, all through the presentation. If they want detail, they will ask.

16. You have to be solid on facts and data, and target them specifically to the points you are making.

17. You must plan ahead for questions they will have, and address them in your talk, as planned content, as well as take them live.

18. Never attempt to cover up or sidestep problems, bad news or sticking points.

Remember, high-pressure executives are a different breed of dog. You have to know how to manage this group, without appearing to manage them. You have to be tolerant of their big egos and tightly-wound tactics and be able to still show that you can take their stress and operate successfully under pressure. You must be flexible and adaptive, on the fly. You must be bottom-line oriented and target your material to their success, at all times.

Finally, prepare so well that you make it seem like you eat, live and breathe your material. This will allow you to be in the moment and intuitively react to the happenings in the room. Do all this, and they will think you are one of them. At least for that hour you are presenting.

Did we get that large training contract in Silicon Valley all those years ago? Well, I was able to salvage the presentation enough to get them to offer us a co-development pilot program with their company. I thought that was a major victory. And I'll tell you one thing. My business partner and I never made those presentation errors again, anytime we spoke to executives. I hope you don't either.

" "

Thoughts About Speaking

Bridge the gap with closed minds though careful dissection of ideas and solid presentation of fact.

Maximillian Degenerez

The most used program in computers and education is PowerPoint. What are you learning about the nature of the medium by knowing how do to a great PowerPoint presentation? Nothing. It certainly doesn't teach you how to think critically about living in a culture of simulation.

Sherry Turkle

When I'm acting, I'm in a different place, singing is the last thing on my mind, and when I'm on stage, there's no acting at all involved, not even presentation, it's just who I am.

Harry Connick, Jr.

How To Be An Effective Moderator And Facilitator

Pitfalls, Personalities And Procedures

If you have ever been recruited to run a meeting, it may have seemed like a pretty simple endeavor at the time. But once you got into the meeting, I'm sure you discovered that there were many subtle and not-so-subtle landmines and surprises along the way. You discovered that some participants actually seemed to enjoy putting up roadblocks and being difficult! Amazing isn't it? You may also have discovered that attempting to orchestrate a group and keep it moving is akin to herding cats. It's a great concept, but the execution is a true challenge. To top it all off, a good moderator or facilitator has a very special skill set. You need the internal constitution of a pit bull, yet with the demeanor of a United Nations diplomat, and the verbal judo skills of a communications black belt.

Here I will give you an overview of what it takes to be a good meetings moderator and facilitator. You will discover the range of skills needed, common errors they make, habits of successful moderators and facilitators, the numerous and varied personalities found in groups, a set of consulting questions to help you target the issues, and an extensive set of comments you can make to orchestrate the group and keep everything flowing smoothly.

This document has five major topic areas that will help demystify the intricacies of meeting dynamics, and give you insight into how to be a more effective moderator and facilitator by using procedural and communication techniques.

1. Errors Moderators And Facilitators Make

2. Habits Of Effective Moderators And Facilitators

3. Personality Types In Groups

4. Consulting-Style Questions That Help Target The Issues

5. Comments Facilitators And Moderators Use To Manage Groups

Key Moderating And Facilitating Skills

Here are the seven major skills you will be using when you run meetings.

1. Reflecting and clarifying using active listening

2. Asking probing or follow-up questions

3. Using silence, to allow people to think and rest mentally

4. Using non-verbal signals (body language)

5. Managing conflict by helping disagreement to be productive

6. Summarizing by briefly stating the main thoughts

7. Shifting gears by moving from one speaker or topic to another

Errors Moderators And Facilitators Make

These mistakes are made from either not knowing what to do, or from not planning for the various scenarios likely to happen in a meeting. As you read these, imagine in your mind what you would do in each situation. Sometimes even though you have diligently set the "ground rules" at the start of the meeting, people will still do what they want to do, or inadvertently break the rules and protocols you've set forth. When these derailers happen you need to gracefully bring people back to the correct pathway.

Here are some of the most common mistakes moderators and facilitators make when they lead meetings.

1. They allow panelist after panelist to drone on well beyond their allotted time.

2. They don't set any ground rules, or make them too complicated, or they are disorganized.

3. They fail to have the names of the players spelled out phonetically, in their notes, and well-practiced.

4. They fail to arrange for proper micing of everyone.

5. They have not orchestrated how questioners will get to a mic.

6. They stick to a rigid, predictable program pattern that becomes boring.

7. They sound formal, and use formulaic introductions of each panelist.

8. They allow each panelist to take over the floor by standing up.

9. They allow audience questioners to actually grab and take the mic.

10. They allow questioners to line up in a row, instead of using a runner with a mic to go to the people.

11. They take over the meeting and make it about them.

12. They give long analyses and ask long questions that bog the energy down.

13. They allow each panelist to introduce themselves, with no time controls.

14. They allow each panelist to speak ad hoc.

15. They make their opening remarks too lengthy.

16. They have not figured out where they will be when they deliver remarks.

17. They allow long questions. Shorter questions are better.

18. They fail to interpret audience questions that are poorly constructed, convoluted, vague, etc.

19. They play favorites with the panelists.

20. They tend to ignore the quieter panelists, who may have much wisdom to share.

21. They are judgmental and critical.

22. They lose interest and that sagging energy infects the group.

23. They are too high-spirited, and that dominance takes over the group and inhibits participation.

Habits Of Effective Moderators And Facilitators

These are some basic operating principles that will help you stay on top of your meetings.

1. Send advance materials that set the proper stage and get people excited and interested.

2. Set the ground rules, housekeeping and tone.

3. Begin with an interesting question to draw people in.

4. Use AIDA: Get their ATTENTION, then their INTEREST, then raise their DESIRE, and finally get them to take ACTION.

5. Demonstrate that you are a careful listener.

6. Show that you have these qualities: Curiosity, neutrality, orchestrator, catalyst, sharp observer, can read the subtext, willing and able to bravely state what you see and hear, don't take things personally, gentle and whimsical sense of humor, able to sense the mood of the group, notice group shifts, flexible and open, think well on your feet, creative, verbally articulate, diffuser of arguments using verbal judo. You need to be very interested, yet detached.

7. Be able to easily and diplomatically cut people off and correct them without them taking it personally.

8. Let the panelists know that your opening question will allow enough time to share their "core, big picture" view of the topic.

9. Attempt to get panelists to talk directly to each other. Don't let them speak only to you or one other person in the group. You want to create an interactive discussion. You can say: Sam, talk to Bob (fellow panelist). See if you can sell him on your viewpoint.

10. Use the acronym GEPO to break stalling, perfectionism or a logjam and stay on track. GEPO stands for Good Enough, Press On.

11. If the audience will ask questions, have them submit written questions to be read out loud by the staff or the moderator. This saves time and insures that the best questions come out. The moderator can also control when these are asked.

12. Use a white board to keep track of comments. Have an additional side board for comments that are off topic, but which may be appropriate for later discussion so the conversation stays on track.

13. Use the verbal construction of "Yes, and..." instead of "Yes, but...". When you use the connecting word 'but', it negates whatever came before it. When you use the connecting word 'and', it joins and continues your thought.

14. Use 'we' more than you use 'you'. That makes people feel they are all in it together. For example, say "We need to move a little faster pace now to get all we need to do done before time runs out".

15. Label the various behavior of participants, particularly early in the meeting, so people understand what is meant by "staying on topic". Point out when various people are too conceptual, too vague, too verbose, etc. Set the tone.

16. Ask everyone for final comments, with a time frame. Give each person a minute or two to add recommendations, future predictions, their take-away, or a summary of the session.

17. Say thank you to everyone at the end. Thank conference organizers and sponsors who helped make the event possible. Lead the applause.

18. Have at least a working knowledge of MBTI (Meyers-Briggs Type Indicator) and group dynamics and the types of roles people play in groups.

Personality Types In Groups

The more you can understand people's motivations, behaviors and operating styles, the better you can manage the room. You can also predict how people will behave based on their "type" or personality profile. Prediction is power. You can plan your responses for predictable types of situations that pop up all the time. Here is a handy list of the different "characters" you will encounter as you moderate your meetings. Every meeting has at least some of these folks in attendance. You can take the approach that you accept people as they are, yet still seek to influence them and manage their behaviors so the meeting can still be run optimally.

1. **Alpha Andy:** He thinks he is the smartest person in the room, city, county, state and universe.

2. **Arguin' Arnie:** He doesn't discuss or converse, he attacks.

3. **Bashful Bob:** He panics if he has to speak in public.

4. **Blackberry Brett:** He and his cell phone are inseparable.

5. **Blocking Biff:** He tosses up roadblocks and limitations for everything.

6. **Bossy Benny:** He thinks he's in charge of everything and everyone.

7. **Braggin' Bert:** He loves talking about his favorite subject—himself.

8. **Butt'n In Betty:** She cuts people off and finishes their sentences.

9. **Chattering Charlie:** He can talk at 200 words a minute, with gusts up to 500.

10. **Challenging Charlene:** She is suspicious of everyone, and calls them on it.

11. **Clever Clem:** He is an inveterate punster and loves the cute turn of phrase.

12. **Complicated Cal:** He asks convoluted and complex questions.

13. **Confused Carrie:** She is permanently lost and can't formulate a question or statement.

14. **Connie Contrarian:** She says and does the opposite of everyone else.

15. **Critical Colleen:** She finds fault with everything and everyone.

16. **Distracting Danny:** He can find many ways to draw attention to himself to derail the group.

17. **Dominating Darlene:** She loves to tell others what to do and say.

18. **Doctor No:** He is against everything the group is for. He never says yes.

19. **Ego Eddie:** He is a self-made man, and worships his creator.

20. **Encouraging Esther:** She supports the group and is the main cheerleader.

21. **Fidgeting Phil:** He can't sit still or keep his hands quiet. Loves to tap pencils.

22. **Fightin' Fred:** He is verbally combative and picks fights.

23. **Funnybone Phyllis:** She finds humor in everything, even when there is none actually there.

24. **Granular Gary:** He loves to get down in the weeds to discuss minutiae.

25. **Harmony Harold:** He wants everyone to get along.

26. **Hostile Hal:** He has a permanent chip on his shoulder, and on the rest of his body.

27. **Indecisive Indira:** She can never make up her mind.

28. **Impetuous Paul:** His motto is Ready!, Fire! Aim!

29. **Ima In N' Out:** She stands up, walks around, leaves the meeting and comes back on her own schedule, often.

30. **Impressive Ivan:** He couches everything he says in order to show off.

31. **Intellectual Ivy:** She graduated from an Ivy league school, and has the vocabulary to prove it, but no one can understand her $25 words.

32. **Know-It-All Nancy:** She is very smart, and she makes sure you know it.

33. **Late Lanny:** He drops into the meeting late anytime he sees fit, and seems not to care.

34. **Literal Larry:** He interprets everything at the concrete, literal level, and has no ability to discern nuance, or emotional tone from others. He's a walking, talking robot.

35. **Lofty Lou:** He has his head in the clouds as he cites philosophical and flowery concepts.

36. **Malingering Marty:** He has imagined (and sometime real) health and medical issues he loves to bring to everyone's attention.

37. **Martyr Mary:** She is rarely competent, and oddly, likes to let people know it.

38. **Micromanaging Mark:** He takes control of everything.

39. **Mind-Reading Matt:** He thinks he knows what others will say about things and makes predictions.

40. **Mumbling Mary:** She speaks quietly, and not very clearly.

41. **Negative Ned:** He has a dark slant on everything and everyone.

42. **One Syllable Sybl:** Trying to get more than a yes, no or maybe out of her is challenge.

43. **Perfectionist Patty:** She must be perfect, correct and in control at all times.

44. **Perry Pleaser:** He needs to be liked by everyone, since he's a bit insecure.

45. **Process Pauline:** She observes and comments on how the group operates.

46. **Procrastinating Pete:** He can never really get going in his questions or comments.

47. **Putdown Perry:** He criticizes and critiques everyone.

48. **Questioning Quentin:** He must know everything before he commits or comments.

49. **Rambling Ron:** He goes on and on and on and on and...

50. **Robert Reader:** He would rather dig into reading matter than contribute.

51. **Sensitive Sammy:** He gets his feelings hurt every few minutes or so.

52. **Sidetalk Tim:** He loves to have sidebar chats.

53. **Silent Sam:** He rarely speaks up, and tries to blend into the background.

54. **Silly Steve:** He is overly playful and takes nothing seriously.

55. **Slow Sarah:** She takes her time with everything.

56. **Slurring Sammy:** He blends all his words together without any pauses so much you canbarelymakeoutasingleword.

57. **Speed-Freak Philip:** He does everything fast and says everything fast.

58. **Sulking Steven:** He pouts, claims things are unfair and gives new meaning to the word petulance.

59. **Surly Shirley:** She has mastered the art of the put down verbally, and, by using body language.

60. **Therapeutic Theo:** He talks about his personal issues and other people's personal issues, and can easily turn any meeting into a group therapy session.

61. **Tommy Tangent:** He strays off topic and wanders away.

62. **Yes-But Barry:** He has a problem with everything someone says or does, saying "I hear you, but..."

Consulting-Style Questions That Help Target The Issues

Here are some questions I use in my consulting practice that you may find useful in leading a group for generating a sharp focus for precisely analyzing and framing an issue.

1. What keeps you awake at night about the situation?

2. What precise aspects are most troubling to you?

3. What would the executive team say the problems are?

4. What would the employees say the problems are?

5. What would the customers say the problems are?

6. What would your vendors say the problems are?

7. What have previous consultants said the problems are?

8. What previous interventions have you tried to solve these problems?

9. Could you alert us to any sensitive areas or hot button issues that we should be aware of, or avoid in designing interventions?

10. How well do your various departments work together?

11. How well do your various functions work together?

12. Is there any We-They energy between groups in the organization?

13. What groups are not respected in the organization?

14. What's out of balance in the organization?

15. What is your vision for the organization?

16. Is this vision a widely communicated one?

17. Where is the resistance to this vision?

18. What do you see as your organization's biggest strengths?

19. What do the executive team see as your organization's biggest strengths?

20. What do the employees see as your organization's biggest strengths?

21. What are the people competencies required for your organization's success?

22. How would conditions improve as a result of your interventions?

23. What does success look like?

24. Ideally, what would you like to accomplish?

25. What would be the difference in the organization if we were successful?

26. How would you recognize the improvement?

27. How would your employees recognize the improvement?

28. How would customers be better served?

29. If you had to set priorities now, what three things must be accomplished?

30. What will happen if these three things do not improve?

31. What will failure in these three things cost your company financially?

32. If you could just wave a magic wand and instantly greatly improve things without regard to cost, feasibility or constraints, what would that look like?

33. What is the impact you seek on return on investment?

34. What is the profitability improvement expected?

35. What is the productivity improvement expected?

36. What is the people attitude and team morale improvement expected?

37. How will you know we've accomplished this objective?

38. Who will be accountable for determining progress, and how will they do so?

39. What information would you need from customers, and in what form?

40. What information would you need from employees, and in what form?

41. What information would you need from management, and in what form?

42. How will the culture be improved?

43. How will the teams be improved?

44. How will the management be improved?

45. What will the impact be on ROI?

46. How will you determine improvements in morale and attitude?

47. How frequently do you need to assess progress and how?

Comments Facilitators And Moderators Use To Manage Groups

The art of verbal judo when managing groups is to "control" the group without appearing to be controlling. People like to be led or inspired, but they don't like to be controlled. When you speak and are the leader of a group you can naturally exert a stronger sense of control, and while you are moderating and facilitating a group you have less direct control. Here are some phrases you can use to manage a group, and keep it flowing.

1. Let me see if I'm hearing you correctly...

2. What I believe you are saying is...

3. So what you just said is...

4. Is what you are saying this...?

5. To be sure I am clear about your last statement, here is what I heard you say.

6. It sounds to me as though we have been talking about a few major themes. They are...

7. Is this discussion helping us achieve our purpose?

8. And how is that working out for you?

9. Before we move on to the next point, I want to add A, B, C.

10. I didn't catch that. Can you repeat the last point?

11. Let me jump in here.

12. I'm going to make a process note.

13. On a scale of 1-10, with 10 being the strongest, how would you rate the seriousness of that issue?

14. If you had a magic wand you could wave over the situation, with no constraints at all, how would the problem be solved?

15. While that is an important point, it's also important to add...

16. We can agree to disagree. Moving on...

17. It seems like you have some real doubts and misgivings about the material we're covering. Do you feel there is absolutely no way this can work?

18. Let's table that for the moment.

19. I'm going to interrupt you for a moment.

20. You recall that I said I would be interrupting. Well here I am now. When I intervene this helps us stay on track. Think of me as a traffic cop directing traffic.

21. It's great that you have a different point of view that is so conceptual and theoretical. For now, let's look at the facts we have in front of us.

22. We already discussed that earlier and reached a consensus. Do you have anything new to add?

23. I know, here I am again butting in, but I really aim to help.

24. I'm going to remind everyone about our process guidelines again.

25. I think I see where you're going with this. Are you saying this? A, B C.

26. It's your turn to speak up and say what you really are thinking. Don't be bashful!

27. There is no right or wrong here, just personal opinions, and we'd love to know yours.

28. We now have good momentum, so let's keep it going with shorter comments.

29. Let's have you and he discuss that offline, if that is ok. We need to move on.

30. We have some good mojo now, let's keep it moving.

31. That's something that can't be changed now, so let's move past it.

32. Let's come back to that.

33. Your opinions are as valid as anyone's, so please let us know what you think.

34. I wish we had more time for that.

35. Let me refer to our ground rules again so we stay moving.

36. Your point is clearly aimed at the person and not the point. Let's keep to the facts and data.

37. Let's park that thought and start a list of other less-urgent issues for later.

38. Let's refer to our written agenda that will help us stay on track.

39. What seems to be at the heart of this issue?

40. Thank you for your comments and ideas. It's time to hear from someone else now.

41. To keep the conversation flowing, can you summarize?

42. So we can move to the next topic, can you make a conclusion? Or a recommendation?

43. What do others think?

44. Time is of the essence today so please wrap up your statements quickly.

45. You're a wealth of knowledge Bob. What are your action points for everyone?

46. Please finish that point you are on now and choose someone to pass it off to.

47. Thanks for your input and for lightening the atmosphere. We have some very serious topics to cover still and since time is at a premium, let's save the humor for later.

48. I'm sure that could be a seminar unto itself, but for now let's finish what we started.

49. Please stay on a very narrow focus for the next few minutes.

50. That's an interesting point. Now let's see what the rest of the group thinks.

51. There is a method to my madness. You'll thank me for being so persistent about staying on topic.

52. Can you summarize your points in one final sentence?

53. We can criticize facts or beliefs, but let's not have any attacks against a person.

54. We have to be careful not to get too esoteric or too lofty here. Please keep comments at the actionable level as much as possible.

55. Who would like to play devil's advocate on that comment of Bob's?

56. You've made your point beautifully. Anything else to conclude with?

57. Let me summarize what Tom just said and ask if anyone has an addition.

58. Have we exhausted this avenue? Time to move on?

59. Let's return to the topics of A, B and C.

60. It is fun to talk about X, but let's stay on topic Y.

61. I know war stories can be very engaging. I'd like to ask that we save those for after the meeting.

62. Thank you, Ted. Do you have anything to add, Mary?

63. We've been focusing on these views, A and B. Does anyone have strong feelings about the other views?"

64. You both seem to have opposing views. On what parts of this are you in agreement?

65. Anyone have an example from their real-world experience?

66. Who would like to argue against what was just said?

67. Let's stick to the facts and avoid ad hominem attacks.

68. Does anyone have another perspective on this?

69. What are the key points here?

70. Who has a different point of view?

71. Do you agree with your colleague?

72. We are getting ahead of ourselves here, so let's slow down a bit.

73. Let's cross that bridge when we get there.

74. Tom, can you take what Bob just said and add to that?

75. Terry, is what you are saying in agreement with what Allan said a moment ago?

76. Say that to Bob and let's see how he reacts.

77. Let's have the two of you have a dialogue on that.

78. What you said seems to contradict what Bob just said. What do you think?

79. Can you give us an example?

80. What do you mean by that?

81. Any exceptions to that rule?

82. How would you implement that?

83. Any roadblocks to getting that done?

84. How have you seen people resist that initiative?

Be Aware And Know Your People

Now you know what to expect as a moderator and facilitator. You have the lay of the land regarding people and situations. You also have a nice armamentarium of phrases to use to help manage the flow of a meeting. Good luck and enjoy the meetings adventure!

❝   ❞

Thoughts About Speaking

Running for me has always been a great place to get away. It's a great stress reliever for me. It's great if I need to be working on something in my mind, whether it's things I need to be memorizing or thinking about, or I have some presentation coming up.

Scott Bakula

The most nerve-wracking experience is an oral presentation in class. And right under that would be doing 'Saturday Night Live' or 'David Letterman.' One of those shows.

Rivers Cuomo

We worry about appearing awkward in a presentation. But up to a point, most people seem to feel more comfortable with less-than-perfect speaking abilities. It makes the speaker more human - and more vulnerable, meaning he is less likely to attack our decisions or beliefs.

John P. Kotter

Speaking To The Media

Running a press conference with the media is a very interesting, some harrowing experience. Speaking one on one with the media is usually more manageable. Here are some strategies you can use for either situation.

1. Start with the end of the conference first. What do you want the newspapers and magazines to write tomorrow? What do you want radio to say? What do you want TV to say and show? Write these statements out. This will be your audience takeaway statement.

2. Write out the questions they may ask.

3. Write out the difficult questions they may ask.

4. Write out the hostile questions they may ask.

5. Create sound bytes.

6. Repeat and paraphrase all questions.

7. Have someone post updates about the conference during the press conference to your Twitter feed or Facebook page.

8. Avoid industry specific jargon. Spell out acronyms once when first used and explain their relevance.

9. Don't assume knowledge in the audience that is not actually there.

10. Take complex and technical concepts and put them into "everyman language" so anyone can understand.

11. When you can't avoid using technical terms, carefully define them.

12. Ask reporters to please state their name and the newspaper, magazine, radio or TV station they represent before asking their question.

13. If you are asked difficult questions you aren't prepared to answer, say, "We aren't prepared to comment on that at this time".

14. Avoid giving speculative answers and don't answer hypothetical questions.

15. Don't be afraid of having some "dead air." The media can and will edit this out in their TV pieces.

16. Don't use the term "off the record. There is no "off the record". The central idea of a press conference is to be "on the record".

17. If someone asks a highly technical question, say you will answer it after the press conference. Otherwise this will ruin the energy and audience engagement.

What Do Reporters Want?

1. Narratives. Stories, human interest.

2. A news hook or tie-in with current events.

3. Stories that are broad enough in scope so they will appeal to a wide audience of their constituency.

4. Stories with conflict. Reporters like protagonists and antagonists they can put against each other in a story arc with drama and intrigue.

5. It is better to be a bit too advanced in your content, than too basic. Audiences will blame themselves for not completely understanding your talk, and blame you for wasting their time with an elementary talk.

" "

Thoughts About Speaking

Debating clubs among boys are very useful, not only as affording pleasant meetings and interesting discussions, but also as serving for training grounds for developing the knowledge and the qualities that are needed in public life.

Annie Besant

One of the things that I did before I ran for president is I was a professional speaker. Not a motivational speaker - an inspirational speaker. Motivation comes from within. You have to be inspired. That's what I do. I inspire people, I inspire the public, I inspire my staff. I inspired the organizations I took over to want to succeed.

Herman Cain

I realized I love motivating and I love empowering and I love inspiring people. I did that as an athlete for 18 years, and I am able to do that as a motivational speaker now as well as doing work on television.

Dominique Dawes

Making Presentations To International Audiences

I have spoken to both international audiences within the US, and I have also spoken outside of the US. Both speaking situations call for careful advance planning, and for situational awareness once at the speaking event. Here are some strategies you can use when you find yourself about to speak to international audiences.

1. Direct and forceful language may often be considered rude in some countries.

2. Volunteers may not volunteer.

3. Do not call on someone unless they have clearly volunteered.

4. Some audiences may greet the call for questions with silence.

5. Due to the time needed for mental translation, an international may take longer to answer a question, even though they may completely understand it.

6. In some cultures, asking a question of an instructor may be seen as a sort of disrespect.

7. Let people save face in all that you do.

8. Humor does not easily translate, so be careful, and judicious in its use.

9. Do not assume that a person with a problem speaking English indicates their inability to understand English.

10. When an international asks for something you said to be repeated, take their request at face

value and repeat what you just said word-for-word. While a native speaker may often want a paraphrase to enhance their understanding, an international is generally asking for another chance to hear the sentence again, so they can understand it, as is. If you change the sentence on them, they will need to begin all over again.

11. When using a translator, add about 25% extra time to your talk.

12. Don't use contractions. Say cannot, instead of can't, for example.

13. Use words for the measurement, weights and currency of the country to which you are speaking.

14. The use of "air quotes" with your fingers can be misinterpreted.

15. Localize your terminology.

16. Don't raise your volume if an international does not understand. Instead, speak the same sentence again, more slowly.

17. Use very few sports references. Use nature references instead, which are more universal.

18. Be aware that words can have vastly different meanings across cultures.

19. All audiences have what is known as "listener lag". This is the delay needed to make sense of what the speaker has said. International's require a longer lag. To effect this, place more space between words, and an even longer pause at the end of sentences. For ends of paragraphs, make that pause huge.

" "

Thoughts About Speaking

I believe that any type of education can be great, but an education about ourselves can create something wonderful. I am a comedian, but people have called me a motivational speaker. I don't really consider myself that at all.

Andy Andrews

Earl Nightingale has inspired more people toward success and fortune than any other motivational speaker on the planet.

Zig Ziglar

The best meeting I ever went to was a meeting in France where the talk slots were 60 minutes long, but you were told to prepare a five-minute talk. It was absolutely great because the entire talk was a conversation between the speaker and the audience.

Tim Hunt

Ways To Wake Up Web Presentations

So now you want to do a webinar. Or maybe you will be doing a speaking gig via the internet. Perhaps you'll be recording your talk using your web cam. Whatever the purpose, web speaking is NOT the same as live, in-person speaking events.

I hear too many webinar presenters begin slowly, blandly, haltingly. They chit chat as people come on line, even if the published start time has passed. This is not good. They say things like, "Before get started...". Well, they HAVE started! You must get the attention of your audience right away. One of the best ways to do that is by using the acronym called AIDA. This is a sales mnemonic where AIDA means Attention, Interest, Desire, Action. To be heard, they need to know you are about to speak-get their attention. The start of your message should create interest to hear more. Next raise their desire to continue listening, and finally, if you have succeeded, they will want to act on your message. In a webinar, get your audience's attention right from the outset: Use humor, tell a short story, post a statistic, give a famous quote, or display a compelling image.

Laptop camera angles are awful. Check this in advance and correct for it. Shooting a camera angle from below is the kiss of death for your image. To make the camera angle look normal, stack your laptop on some wide, sturdy hardback books, so it is at eye height.

Make sure what the camera catches behind you is intentional and pleasing. Use a poster, artwork or bookcase. Make sure if you have glass walls behind you that no one will be walking around, on camera. Add your corporate branding. For less than $100 you can add your company logo on a video background banner.

Stay mentally tuned in the entire time: You may become distracted by seeing the webinar chat box, or audience polling data, or by your own email. Don't let that happen. If you have a moderator, let them deal with all that so you can stay focused on your delivery.

Remember you have a real audience. Doing a webinar can feel sterile and remote, since you are not seeing any real faces, so there can be a tendency to relax and give the program with less intensity. Your audience can feel that. Step your energy up by sitting tall (or by standing, walking if not using a camera) so your voice energy reflects your physicality. One trick voice actors and broadcasters use is to post a photo of a person that represents their audience. They then speak to THAT person. This does positively change the emotion in your delivery.

Don't use standard presentation graphic program templates and themes. Everyone has seen it all by now. Instead, be creative and make your own styles.

Here are some strategies you can use right away to give better presentations on the web.

1. Use a series of looping slides as a vamping mechanism, before you begin, as people come into the webinar. These could include:

2. Create a welcome banner with program title and presenter's names and photos.

3. Logistics details and contact information in case there are problems.

4. Conference dial in number and password.

5. Learning objectives for the program.

6. Describe how your audience will interact with you. Will there be phone muting? Will they be able to speak with you via email? Will there be polling? Will they get these results?

7. Make sure your You/I/We ratio is correct. People tune into the mental radio station named WIFFM: What's In It For Me. Use the form of you most of all. If you say, "most people", or "we should", or "one should", your audience tunes out. But once they hear you say "You can improve your marketing approach..." they perk right up, because now they know you are speaking directly to them.

8. Never present a slide with all that you will say, in advance, or your audience will read them, and disengage from what you are saying. Build each point on the slides as you speak.

9. Create some initial rapport with your photo posted while you introduce yourself, or while someone else introduces you.

10. Consider using a single photo on a slide, and then talk about that image. The typical Steve Jobs style was one screen shot or graphic, and maybe a word or phrase at a font size of 60 points.

11. Never read the words on your slides. Your audience may feel insulted. Instead, give context or a new slant to what the slide says. Better still, what you say should be supported by the slide. The best slides add emotion to the words, by use of powerful images.

12. Have higher energy than usual. Stand as you speak to increase your energy. Sit tall in your chair. Use a headset to allow your hands to be active so your voice sounds lively.

13. Use slide sharing.

14. Share your own screen.

15. Ask rhetorical questions often.

16. Take questions as you go, instead of just at the end, so people hear a variety of voices, and you continue to take the pulse of the audience.

17. Avoid "slide show language". Instead of saying "You can see that slide #24 says that...", say instead "There's a color graphic here that will show you..."

18. Look at the camera above the screen, not the screen.

19. Test the camera picture before you go live.

20. Use a telephone headset so you are heard clearly and you don't need to strain towards the mic on the computer to be heard.

21. Make sure your camera sees the background you desire. You may want to use a blue screen or blanket or chair screen to block any unwanted background views. Make sure your viewers see you as a professional.

22. Make sure you have a light source in front of you so that your face is lit. This could be natural light through a window or a lamp. Light from behind or the side casts odd shadows.

23. Plan for changes in natural light from outside if your presentation goes into the latter part of the day, when sunlight diminishes. Have artificial light sources ready.

24. Wear camera-friendly clothes. Wear few patterns or all-white.

25. Reduce and slow your movements to account for camera picture delay.

26. Use a placeholder still photo of you if needed in an emergency.

27. Make sure you are not on camera too much.

28. Turn the camera back on you for Q and A.

29. Burst the content. Do this with audio and visuals. Make your voice and graphics compelling.

30. Use short video clips of interviews.

31. Use two or more presenters for variety and the novelty effect to take place.

32. Use hyperlinks your audience can access.

33. Use an audience poll in advance, with a service like SurveyMonkey.com.

34. Use an audience poll during the talk, with an assistant collating the results.

35. Use a "one slide per minute" pace. More slides and less time per slide keeps things moving.

36. Minimize bullet points per slide.

37. Replace bullet points with photos, graphics and questions.

38. Use a tease. Mention "What is to come later" and keep your audience in suspense.

39. Use "common questions" to get Q and A rolling. Say, "A common question I am asked about this is…".

40. Use the Guy Kawasaki 10-20-30 Rule. That's a PowerPoint show that has only ten slides, lasts no longer than 20 minutes and has text no less than 30-point font.

41. Maintain program pace by slide frequency, not by talking pace.

42. Try one word per slide and talk to that word.

Web casting or speaking via the web can be very interesting. You should not approach it the same way as you would for an on-person event. You have to make adjustments and be aware of what you're doing. Use this checklist as a consultation tool before you create your web presentation.

❝ ❞

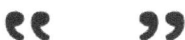

Thoughts About Speaking

I'm less shy now than I was as a kid. After Flight 1549, my family and I had to become public figures and more complete versions of ourselves. I had to teach myself to become an effective public speaker.

Chesley Sullenberger

Oh, I would love to be a motivational speaker. I have pulled myself out of a million potholes, and I can see the potholes ahead of me. That doesn't mean that I could always do that so perfectly for my own life. I totally fall in potholes.

Drew Barrymore

I love a finished speaker, I really, truly do I don't mean one who's polished, I just mean one who's through.

Richard Armour

15 Tips For Making Better Telephone Presentations

Do you use the telephone to conduct teleseminars? If so, this type of speaking is very different from regular in-person speaking. Communicating your policies and expectations is key.

Here are some strategies you can use that will make a difference.

1. **Describe how your audience will interact with you.** Will there be phone muting? Will they be able to speak with you via email? Will there be polling? Will they get these results?

2. **Send a document in advance:** This gives the audience some advance work, and also helps them follow you as you speak. Never read the document word for word. Summarize, add stories and examples, and embellish what they have in their hands.

3. **Make sure you have excellent quality audio equipment:** That includes a high-quality head set or handset, or microphone if you will be using non-video Skype or VOIP. Using a headset ensures that you are heard clearly, and you won't need to strain towards the mic on the computer to be heard.

4. **Test in advance:** If you are recording the teleseminar, make sure you test the sound quality well in advance by recording a practice teleseminar.

5. **Make sure your You/I/We ratio is correct:** People tune into the mental radio station named WIFFM: What's In It For Me. Use the form of you

most of all. If you say, "most people", or "we should", or "one should", your audience tunes out. But once they hear you say "You can improve your marketing approach..." they perk right up, because now they know you are speaking directly to them.

6. **Use the sales mnemonic called AIDA:** AIDA stands for Attention, Interest, Desire, Action. To be heard, they need to know you are about to speak-get their attention. The start of your message should create interest to hear more. Next raise their desire to continue listening, and finally, if you have succeeded, they will want to act on your message. Get your audience's attention right from the outset: Use humor, tell a short story, post a statistic, give a famous quote, or ask a compelling question.

7. **Remember you have a real audience:** Doing a teleseminar can feel sterile and remote, since you are not seeing any real faces, so there can be a tendency to relax and give the program with less intensity. Your audience can feel that. Step your energy up by sitting tall (or by standing, walking if not using a camera) so your voice energy reflects your physicality. One trick voice actors and broadcasters use is to post a photo of a person that represents their audience. They then speak to THAT person. This does positively change the emotion in your delivery.

8. **Have higher energy than usual:** Stand as you speak to increase your energy. Sit tall in your chair. Use a headset to allow your hands to be active so your voice sounds lively.

9. **Ask rhetorical questions often:** Anytime you ask a question that re-engages your audience if they have been drifting away.

10. **Take questions as you go, instead of just at the end:** This way people hear a variety of voices, and you continue to take the pulse of the audience.

11. **Use two or more presenters:** Having two or more people adds vocal variety, and every time a voice changes the novelty effect takes place. The novelty effect states that when the listener hears something change, they reorient to that new stimulus.

12. **Use an audience poll:** You can use a poll in advance, with a service like SurveyMonkey.com.

13. **Use an audience poll during the talk:** Here your assistant can collate the results.

14. **Use a tease:** Mention "What is to come later" and keep your audience in suspense.

15. **Use "common questions" to get Q and A rolling:** Say, "A common question I am asked about this is...", and then answer your own question.

So now you know enough to do a great job presenting on the telephone. I bet you can't wait.

❝   ❞

Thoughts About Speaking

As any speaker will tell you, when you address a large number of people from a stage, you try to make eye contact with people in the audience to communicate that you're accessible and interested in them.

Simon Mainwaring

If I hadn't spent many years trying to be as compassionate as Mother Teresa, as positive a thinker as W. Clement Stone, as prolific a writer as Stephen King, and as good a speaker as many of the legends I have studied, I would not be as successful as I am today.

Jack Canfield

If the speaker won't boil it down, the audience must sweat it out.

Raymond Duncan

Are You A Prisoner of PowerPoint?

The Top Ten Ways Speakers Harm Their Presentations Through Technology

As a professional speaker who also provides presentation coaching to professional speakers and salespeople, I have either seen or made probably all the speaking technology gaffs that exist. I've seen speakers use the wrong technology, use it the wrong way and at the wrong times. But by far, the biggest and most common audience complaint about speakers using technology has got to be--They Overdo It!

Technology can be great. It can bring some Hollywood razzle-dazzle into otherwise tedious presentation material. But many speakers abuse their technology quota. Here I want to help you understand the pitfalls of PowerPoint and the terrors of technology so you don't alienate your audiences.

Here are the top ten most common complaints audiences have about how speakers use high-tech in their presentations.

1. It was too much for too long-- too much of anything is boring.

2. The speaker read the slides too much. We can do that ourselves.

3. The technology gave the talk, so who needs the speaker?

4. It insulted the audience using so much technology.

5. The print was so small, it was really frustrating to follow.

6. The charts were too busy, and we lost sight of the main points.

7. The speaker did not practice their technology and botched it up on stage.

8. The low room light put the audience to sleep.

9. The style and purpose of the talk did not lend itself to technology.

10. The high tech format painted the speaker as needlessly nerdy.

Why do people attend presentations when they don't have to? In hopes of having an experience. Of seeing or learning something they can't get at home. That experience is YOU, the speaker. If they simply wanted the data content, you could send them your PowerPoint slides by email. That would save everyone time and money.

A real live speaker should beat technology or reading a report any day. People enjoy unpredictable theater, and that's what you can give them, if you allow your personality and charisma to shine through on stage.

Why Speakers Fear Stopping Or Reducing Presentation Technology

1. Speakers are afraid to change. They:

2. Have always done it that way.

3. Use it as a crutch, to read from.

4. Can hide as the audience focuses on the technology, not them.

5. Think they alone will not be enough to keep the audience interested.

6. Think that the MTV generation and the Just Do It generation want things fast, to remain fascinated.

Maybe people don't want the attention-deficit type performances speakers think they need to provide. They want the human touch instead.

The Advantages Of Low Or No Technology

1. Fewer or no technical breakdowns and glitches.

2. Less to buy, pack, carry and set up/tear down.

3. Less to be stolen or be misplaced in travel.

4. You will improve your content, vocal and physical messages.

5. Your audience and you can focus on each other more.

6. You won't be like all the other speakers that are technology-heavy.

7. You can craft more creative ways to have fun and connect with your audience.

Have I convinced you to reduce the tech? To go high-touch? To personalize your talks? I hope so.

I urge you to create presentations with either low or no tech and see how your audience responds. See how you present differently. To do this, call a coach. Read some books. Watch top speakers who don't use much tech. Do something to turn off the tech before your audiences turn you off.

❝   ❞

Thoughts About Speaking

There are good leaders who actively guide and bad leaders who actively misguide. Hence, leadership is about persuasion, presentation and people skills.

Shiv Khera

Thaw with her gentle persuasion is more powerful than Thor with his hammer. The one melts, the other breaks into pieces.

Henry David Thoreau

Persuasion is often more effectual than force.

Aesop

INFLUENCING SKILLS
IN SPEAKING

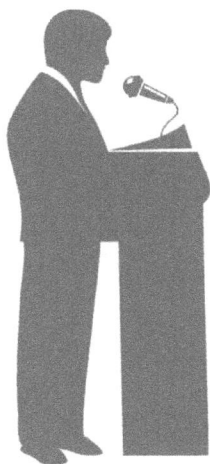

Influence To Win: How Persuasive Are You?

How effectively do you motivate people to buy your services and products? Would you consider yourself a master influencer of people? Do you consider selling more of an art or a science? How often do you sell your ideas from the platform? Every time!

Psychologist Dr. Robert Cialdini wrote the well-known social science book of six laws of persuasion entitled *Influence: The Psychology of Persuasion*, in 1984. Since then the book has steadily accelerated towards classic status. Some say it's already arrived. Indeed, Amazon.com has called the book "Arguably the best book ever on what is increasingly becoming the science of persuasion."

The Six Laws Of Influencing

Cialdini does not call these laws psychological tricks, but as you come to understand these laws as methods of marketing, you will be able to more readily defend yourself from any marketing onslaught that abuses these techniques. Here is the basis of how these laws work. We are constantly looking for short cuts to speed up the countless decisions that must be made in life. We therefore seek out cues, signals and information to cut down on the complexity in life. They help us make mental shorthand out of our world. Know how these laws operate and your operating power with people increases dramatically.

1. Consistency. People have a strong need to be consistent with themselves, in their thoughts, actions and feelings. If someone gives you their word, they will want to keep it, or risk appearing inconsistent, less than reliable, or worse, less than honest. This is why getting customers to agree with you multiple times is so powerful. They say "Yes" So often, when it comes time to close them, how can they suddenly say "No"?

2. Reciprocation. Build a sense of indebtedness in the other person. They will feel a strong urge to reciprocate to make the imbalance even out. That's why salespeople give out free samples, so the customer's unconscious desire to equalize the unbalance is stealthily fulfilled.

3. Social Proof. Why do you always see the tip jar so full at every Starbucks you enter? Is it because people who visit that particular store are so generous? Or because the baristas are so wonderful and deserving of tips? Maybe both. A more likely reason is that the store manager stuffs the tip jar before the store opens, so people get the idea that they should tip a lot. That's social proof in action: Others have tipped generously, and so should I.

4. **Authority.** If a celebrity you admire recommends a product, you are far more likely to purchase that product because you trust and like the celebrity. Your decision becomes a no-brainer. My hero likes it. Therefore I like it.

5. **Liking.** It's amazing how every car salesperson you meet is from your hometown. Or how advertisers only use good-looking models. Why? We like those who are like us (from our home town), and who are pleasing to look at. Both these factors result in more sales.

6. **Scarcity.** "I have only one open slot left all this week. Want me to hold that for you?" You bet. Can you imagine your reaction if the salesperson said, "I'm wide open. I don't have any clients at all. When do you want to come in?" Commodities whither. Scarcity sells.

Persuade others for good reasons. Influence people so their lives are better. Use *The Psychology Of Persuasion* to sell your ideas more, sell better and sell faster than you ever have before. May you become a more powerful persuader and a star on the platform.

❝   ❞

Thoughts About Speaking

The finest eloquence is that which gets things done.

David Lloyd George

Eloquence is a painting of the thoughts.

Blaise Pascal

Play is our brain's favorite way of learning.

Dianne Ackerman

Best Practices
In Platform Persuasion

There is only one reason to get up in front of an audience and speak. Your goal is to have them change their thinking, change how they feel or to act differently. You are attempting to MOVE your audience. You want to CHANGE your audience. You want them to come along with you as you take them on a ride into your imagination.

How will you accomplish this feat? Influencing strategies! You will learn and apply cutting edge psychology of influencing techniques to your speaking. Do this and your reputation as a motivational, powerful speaker will grow dramatically.

First, let's look at ten major mistakes speakers make in attempting to influence their audiences.

Ten Persuasion Mistakes Speakers Make From The Platform

1. They have a heavy reliance on statistics and numbers. They bore people and create no emotional connection. Numbers are for the mind only.

2. They use information dumping, a fate worse than death.

3. They lecture. This is old school and the kiss of death.

4. They engage in "Death by PowerPoint".

5. They turn the lights off during their slide shows.

6. They repeat things without variation. Instead, break things up often. Novelty is the KING of mental stimulation.

7. They don't understand psychology. People don't agree, buy or change because they are MADE to understand. People change because they feel understood.

8. They are too slick. Fast-talking, covering-up the details and attempts to coerce only lead to distrust and sabotage after the fact, even if people agree with you at first.

9. They seek perfection. Audiences don't need perfection. They want humanity. Technically-perfect presentations can be devoid of any humanity.

10. They are too predictable. Well-organized and orchestrated presentations that are information driven miss the human element and the element of "theater", and surprise. Don't be too predictable.

Now we will examine the best ways to influence your audiences.

Best Practices In Platform Persuasion

1. Have the mindset that ALL speeches are for ONE reason only--to persuade.

2. Tell stories that raise the emotions of the audience, and ones that tug at their heartstrings.

3. Ask yourself, "What am I offering my audience that they could NOT get if they read the book, saw the PowerPoint or got the lecture notes in email? Then focus on that.

4. Audiences are incredibly curious about who the speaker is as a person. Share yourself with them. Let them see the real you, not just a business persona.

5. YOU are the message. Be congruent and you will be convincing.

6. LOSE YOURSELF in your passion for your topic, and in your desire to help your audience learn it.

7. Show your audience your POINT OF VIEW. Let them know how you FEEL about your topic. Then they will feel it too.

8. No audience cares how much you know until they know how much you care.

9. Influence comes from an emotional transfer between the speaker and the audience.

10. People buy (are influenced) on emotion, and they justify their purchase (decision to agree) with logic, so their thoughts are consistent with their feelings and actions.

11. Ask for the sale when you speak. Ask your audience to take on new mindsets, think about things differently, take new courses of action and change habit patterns.

12. Speak directly to their needs and wants, not YOUR agenda.

13. Be audience-centered, not speaker-centered. Focus on making the entire presentation listener friendly.

14. Grab control of the minds of your audience members by asking questions.

15. Use audience-interactive and audience-involvement techniques that draw the listener in to active participation.

16. Continually tune your audience into the radio station WIIFM (What's In It For Me?). Make your material relevant and they will respond.

17. Use a Socratic Selling approach. Ask questions, get them talking and discover how much they know. Let them convince themselves on your issues as you ask thoughtful questions designed to lead them to a clear conclusion.

18. Use mnemonics to help your audience remember and organize your material.

19. Presenting BOTH sides of an argument adds to your credibility, and thus, your believability.

20. Remove all DISQUALIFIERS that harm your credibility. Examples to remove would be basic, easily-avoided errors in grooming, dress and manners that offend.

21. Presenters are concerned about their hands, that audiences will be observing them. True, but what's worse than fidgeting hands are flitting and darting eyes. Excess scanning, and the inability to connect visually with the audience leads to lack of trust and hence believability.

22. Make sure YOU can state your premise, your essence, your purpose, your REASON for giving the speech. That guides the organization of your material. If YOU can't summarize why you are speaking, the AUDIENCE won't be able to either!

23. People don't argue with their own data (and conclusions about the data). Construct experiences for them that will get them thinking and coming to logical conclusions about things.

They will remember these far more than you telling them.

24. Just as you SELL to personality types, you should speak to the personality of your audiences. You need far less supporting reasons and motivators for an audience of CEO's than you do for a group of front line customer service folks. The CEO's are very bottom line oriented and like to decide fast and move to the next topic.

25. Customize to your audience's learning preferences. This includes learning styles, ages, gender, cultures, values, etc.

26. Be attuned to your audience's hot buttons, current mindsets, organizational dynamics, and topical issue locally, regionally and nationally.

27. Vary your EVIDENCE with five styles:

    - Stories (the brain encodes/remembers these like actual experiences)
    - Analogy and metaphor
    - Expert comments and research studies
    - Statistics and facts
    - Real life examples

28. Use the "three proofs of Aristotle":

    - Ethos: ethics and credibility
    - Pathos: passion
    - Logos: logic and reason

Influencing is as much an art as it is a science. Use the science behind the art to beguile your audiences and to delight them with how you convince them of your ideas. If your ideas help them and fit them, people will gladly follow you anywhere.

❝   ❞

Thoughts About Speaking

Self education is, I firmly believe,
the only kind of education there is.

Isaac Asimov

The essence of teaching is to make learning
contagious, to have one idea spark another.

Marva Collins

It is the supreme art of the teacher to awaken
joy in creative expression and knowledge.

Albert Einstein

CHECKLISTS AND FORMS FOR SPEAKERS

Pre-Program Speaking Questionnaire (PPQ)

Hello _____,

Thanks again for all your help.

I am really looking forward to meeting you and the other attendees at the _____ Program. To help me customize the program I was wondering if you could complete as much of this questionnaire as you think would be relevant. I really appreciate your help!

If it's easier, you may just want to send this back via email with comments in the spaces provided. Alternatively, I would be happy to phone you for a brief chat to fill the form out together.

Thanks again!

Best Regards,

Bill Cole

This pre-program questionnaire is for Bill Cole's presentation to your group on

_____.

We need your help!! Me would like to specifically meet your needs with my presentation. Please take a few moments and help us.

We have filled out the answers to the questions below to the best of our knowledge. Please double check our answers and make additions and corrections. Fill in the questions we left blank. We were uncertain of this

information and thought it best for you to provide it to
us.

Return this questionnaire to:
William B. Cole Consultants
19925 Stevens Creek Blvd.
Suite 100
Cupertino, CA 95014-2358 USA

Or email it to Bill@MentalGameCoach.com No later than
_____

If you have any questions, call 408-725-7291, or fax
408-440-2398.

Presentation title:

Possible Talk Themes:

Conference/meeting theme?

What is the specific purpose of this meeting (awards
banquet, annual meeting etc.)?

What is the theme of this specific meeting?

What are you hoping to accomplish with this meeting?

Why do you think I'll be an asset to this meeting?

What are you hoping to accomplish with my particular program?

How will you know if my program is successful? Please give me a target.

Are there any particular topics or ideas that I should address during my program?

Are there any sensitive issues that should be avoided?

Date   Start time

End time   Breaks?

What is on the program just before I speak?

Will I be able to have some staging set-up time right before I speak?

If I go on right after another speaker, or with no staging set-up time due to program restrictions, when can I arrive to set up my staging area?

What happens on the program right after I speak?

When does your meeting begin? (date and time)

When does it end? (date and time)

Audience dress code for the meeting?

Do you want me to write an article for your newsletter or other publications prior to my program?

What is your desired program mix?

% Motivation

% How To/Nuts & Bolts

What is the audience's overall opinion regarding the subject of my presentation? (favorable, hostile, neutral?)

Please list some industry-specific terms, phrases, jargon or acronyms that I might incorporate into my program.

Please list any humorous buzz-words, pet peeves or inside jokes in your industry or organization I might use for humorous material.

Please share any "local color" (humorous goings-on) you may be aware of relating to the location where my program will be held.

Introducer's name and title?

Work Phone

Meeting-site phone

E-mail

Would someone be able to assist me just before my program ends in collecting program evaluations in return for a raffling of a valuable prize?

Is there any publicity work I can do for you while I am at your event? Radio or television? Please let us know ahead of time, so we can arrange travel.

Who are the other speakers on the program?

Speaker

Topic

Speaker

Topic

Speaker

Topic

What speakers have you used in the past that covered topics related to the material I will be presenting to you?

What professional speakers have you used in the past and what did they speak on?

What did you like and/or dislike? Without their names if you would like, but please comment on the material they used.

Name three main movers and shakers of your group that will be in my audience. With your permission we would like to contact them for more information on your group.

Name

Phone

Name

Phone

Name

Phone

What would make my presentation really "special" for your group?

The Audience Demographics

Number attending?

% Female?

% Male?

% of Guests?

Spouses attending?

Average age of attendees?

Annual average income?

Income range?

Educational background?

Major job responsibilities of audience?

% Senior executives:

% Board of directors

% Admin./clerical

% Mid-management

% Officers/sales reps

% Entrepreneurs

Ethnic diversity?

% Caucasian

% Hispanic

% Black

% Asian

% Other

Positions/Job Titles?

Details About Your Audience

Is their attendance at your meeting mandatory?

At my program?

Will attendees be charged a fee for attending?

If so, what amount?

Please describe what the audience will be doing in the hour preceding my program.

What will they be doing after my program?

What should I know about the people in your group before I start my program? Are there any problems, competition, resentment or peer pressure that I should be aware of?

Their challenges?

Their breakthroughs?

What are the most significant things on their minds as they come to this meeting?

Are there any hearing or sight-impaired individuals who will attend my program?

What separates your high performance people from others?

Tell Us About Your Industry

Problems?

Challenges?

Breakthroughs?

Tell Us About Your Organization

Problems?

Challenges?

Breakthroughs?

What are the greatest accomplishments of this group?

What are the current projects of this group?

Significant events? Mergers? Relocations?

Will my presentation be audiotaped and/or videotaped?

333

If you wish, I will make my educational materials available to your audience, so that they may continue the learning process at home. There are two ways this can be arranged. Please check the one that is most appropriate for your group.

A. _____ Group purchase in advance for each attendee, at wholesale.

☐ Deliver before the program

☐ Deliver at the end of the program

B. _____ Materials made available at the back of the room after the presentation.

If you checked "B", please make sure that:

Nothing will be on the program directly after my presentation and that there will be a break for at least 20 minutes.

A table will be made available for me to place my materials by the exit door.

Someone from your group will assist with sales.

Travel Information

Location of presentation and venue name

What time can we get into the room to set up?

Who would the contact person be to allow us entry?

Address

Phone

Location at the site itself?

Airport to arrive at

How will I be transported from the airport to your site?

Taxi?

Rental car?

Pick-up person?

My own vehicle?

Pick-up person's name?

Phone

If an emergency occurs on the way to the site, who would be an alternate contact if you are unavailable?

Name and title

Business phone

Home phone

On-site phone

Pager

What is your organization's WEB SITE address?

We can provide free articles for your web site, ezine or hard-copy newsletter. What topics would you like? (For an overview, see our web site).

What deadlines do you have for inclusion of these articles?

On the web site?

For your e-zine?

For your hard-copy publications?

What is YOUR e-mail address?

Thank you very much for your help in making our presentation a success!! We are looking forward to working with you closely to make sure everyone has a good time and leaves the program with valuable information.

Bill Cole, MS MA

PS--Please send us any printed information on your group that may help us such as:

1. Corporate reports
2. Association magazine/newsletter
3. Key product brochures
4. News releases on this presentation
5. Informative articles
6. Past convention programs
7. This presentation's program/brochure

8. Service recognition programs
9. Organization chart
10. Service standards
11. Staff/company newsletter
12. Mission/vision/values
13. Training programs-table of contents
14. Sample sales tracking reports
15. Special promotions/campaigns
16. Meeting agenda/invitation
17. Service measurement tools
18. Sample completed performance appraisal
19. Strategic plan/objectives
20. Business/marketing plan
21. Job descriptions
22. Customer/member newsletter

❝ ❞
Thoughts About Speaking

Nine-tenths of education is encouragement.

Anatole France

The mind is not a vessel to be filled but a fire to be kindled.

Plutarch

When planning for a year, plant corn.
When planning for a decade, plant trees.
When planning for life, train and educate people.

Chinese Proverb

Pre-Program Welcome And Questionnaire To Attendees

Dear Attendee,

I am looking forward to your participation in my April 25th presentation, The Mental Game Of Speaking: Peak Performance For Presenters. This program will focus on how to achieve peak performance. We will not directly address platform mechanics, staging, topic development or speech construction. What we will learn, however, is how to be more polished, more at ease and more connected to our audience and to bring forth our best performances more often, when we need them most.

Here are some questions for you to review and bring with you (in your head or on paper) to the presentation. Your answers can remain private if you wish, but please read these questions now, so the presentation has more meaning for you. If you wish, you may send these to me in advance.

1. How do you define peak performance on the platform?

2. How would you rate yourself in your ability to handle speaker's nerves?

3. What approaches have you used in your attempts to handle speaker's nerves?

4. Which ones have worked?

5. Which ones have not worked?

6. What system do you use now to achieve inspired, top-level performance when you speak?

7. Describe your best performance when speaking. What was that experience like?

8. Describe your worst performance when speaking. What was that experience like?

Please answer the following questions and return to Bill Cole by fax, e-mail or snail mail prior to the program.

1. What about the art of performing do you hope to learn?

2. What performance tools and skills do you want to leave with?

3. What is your background in attending presentation skills trainings?

4. What is your experience level as a speaker? (Starting, 5 years, 10 years, veteran, etc.)

5. What is your background in any type of peak performance, sport psychology, stress management or self-improvement training?

Wear comfortable clothing on April 25th. We will be active with indoor games and group

experiences. The room is large, so bring extra layers just in case. Food and drink will be provided, so if you will be unable to attend, please let us know as far in advance as possible to make the head count accurate and to help reduce costs.

There will be plenty of break time for networking so bring your elevator speech and lots of business cards! Also, bring at least one humorous platform performance experience to share that either happened to you, or that you observed as an audience member.

Please let me know how I can make your participation more valuable and rewarding. I am looking forward to seeing you!!

Best Regards,

Bill

Bill Cole, MS, MA
William B. Cole Consultants
19925 Stevens Creek Blvd.
Suite 100
Cupertino, CA 95014-2358 USA
VOICE: 408-725-7191
TOLL FREE: 888-445-0291
FAX: 408-440-2398
Bill@MentalGameCoach.com
http://www.MentalGameCoach.com

❝   ❞

Thoughts About Speaking

The only person who is educated is the one who has learned how to learn and change.

Carl Rogers

The best teachers are the best storytellers. We learn in the form of stories.

Frank Smith

The mediocre teacher tells. The good teacher explains. The superior teacher demonstrates. The great teacher inspires.

William Arthur Ward

The Trade Program

Many speakers use a unique strategy for getting new clients and other benefits called a "trade program". In return for a free brief talk, you will receive numerous benefits, and you'll hope to sell the firm on your services, in addition to providing them with an immediately useful and entertaining program. This is a showcase, and a barter arrangement in essence.

As an emerging professional speaker, this may be one of your best avenues for getting work. Even though you don't get paid money for doing this, at the very least, you can receive goods, services and benefits that add to up to significant value, almost as good as cash:

1. Testimonials

2. Practice

3. A venue to test new material with a live audience

4. Their name for your client list

5. Insights about yourself as a speaker

6. A chance to sell yourself in front of decision-makers

7. Leads for more clients

8. Possible coaching clients

9. Product sales

10. Mailing list of attendees to whom you can market

11. Talk evaluation by all attendees (This is the sheet where the audience will give you testimonials).

12. Audio and/or videotape of your session

13. Space to put your articles in their publications

Here's the letter. You can have your friend or contact, who is in this target business, contact their boss and then you will set up the free talk and go from there.

Be sure to put in writing whatever trade or barter items you want in return for the talk. Here is a sample letter.

Date

Mr. Steve Somebody
Some Name Business
554 Name Avenue
Silicon Valley, CA 95128

Dear Steve,

It was a pleasure speaking with you on the telephone recently about your business. This letter will confirm that I will be speaking to your group on Thursday, October 21, at your luncheon for approximately 45 minutes in San Jose.

I am a coach who helps individuals and organizations raise the bar on peak performance in their professional and personal lives. I offer a limited number of complimentary presentations on peak performance to organizations every year and am happy to extend this offer to your group.

I am offering this presentation to selected businesses to assist me in gathering new material for my next book, in progress, The Mental Game Of Selling. This presentation will add immediate value to your people's productivity. If my presentation makes sense for your people, and I can offer your organization genuine value, we can discuss furthering our relationship at a later time.

In return for my doing a needs assessment for your group, delivering a customized 45 minute presentation, program handouts, conducting an email follow-up with attendees, and providing you with an article for your newsletter or ezine, I would receive the following:

- A five-minute one-page written evaluation by each audience member on my one-page form that I supply.
- A letter of thanks from your organization on your letterhead.
- Granting the use of your company name on my client list.
- A group photograph with the attendees.
- Names of organizations and contact people you would recommend I contact for additional programs.
- Audio and videotape capabilities to tape my program.

I am really looking forward to meeting everyone and to delivering an exciting, valuable program for your company.

Sincerely,

Bill Cole, MS, MA
President

Attached:

- Pre-program questionnaire
- Room set-up form
- Press kit
- Photo for your newsletter and website
- Article for your newsletter and website

" "

Thoughts About Speaking

I think education is power. I think that being able to
communicate with people is power. One of my main
goals on the planet is to encourage people to
empower themselves.

Oprah Winfrey

I have come to believe that a great teacher is a great
artist and that there are as few as there are any other
great artists. Teaching might even be the greatest of the
arts since the medium is the human mind and spirit.

John Steinbeck

A teacher affects eternity; he can never
tell where his influence stops.

Henry Adams

Speaking Program Action Checklist

Bill Cole, MS, MA

Client _____

Program Title _____

Location _____

Date _____

Time and Length _____

Contact Person and Title _____

Business Phone _____

Cell Phone _____

E-Mail _____

Billing Address _____

Web site _____

Pre-Program

Date Completion   Date Completed

Required   or Confirmed

Contracts And Finances

- [ ] Speaking fees one sheet sent
- [ ] Speaking trade-outs one sheet sent
- [ ] Agreement sent
- [ ] Agreement received
- [ ] Agreement signed by both parties and returned to each
- [ ] Invoice for deposit sent
- [ ] Deposit of $_____ received, on date: _____
- [ ] Taxi/shuttle to airport-San Jose
- [ ] Taxi/shuttle from airport-San Jose
- [ ] Taxi/shuttle to airport-at hotel
- [ ] Taxi/shuttle from airport-at hotel
- [ ] Plane tickets-you make and get reimbursed
- [ ] Plane tickets-host makes and gets reimbursed
- [ ] Other transportation
- [ ] Car rental
- [ ] Parking fees
- [ ] Hotel billed directly to host
- [ ] Hotel will be reimbursed to you
- [ ] Hotel reservations confirmed
- [ ] Food, per diem, no receipts.
- [ ] Copies for handouts if you print

☐ Postage/mailing for handouts if you mail

☐ Expenses NOT to invoice: list- Tips for travel, in hotel

☐ Expense receipts gathered/credit card statements

☐ Invoice for expenses sent

☐ Check for expenses received

☐ Check available in person after program

Promotions

☐ Promotional materials sent/directed to web site

☐ Photo ☐ Bio

☐ Articles ☐ Testimonials

Travel

☐ Taxi reservation made

☐ Plane reservations made

☐ Airport parking reservation made

☐ Hotel confirmation received

☐ Hotel shuttle confirmation received

☐ Handouts To Helpers

☐ PPQ sent

☐ PPQ returned

☐ Contact with introducer made

☐ Introduction sent to introducer

☐ Room set-up sent

Handouts

Attendee's materials sent to:

☐ Hotel ☐ Client

☐ Other _____

☐ Attendee's materials duplicated by client

☐ Your extra handouts carried by you

Your Products

☐ Your books

☐ Your CD's

Your Equipment

☐ Your equipment

☐ Your Olympus digital recorder

☐ Props, posters and magic items

Your Notes

☐ Your notes you take on stage

☐ Your extra handouts

☐ Your extra handouts

☐ Your extra handouts

Post Program

☐ Testimonial letter request sent to client

☐ Testimonial letter received

☐ Letter for request for referrals sent to client

- [ ] Letter for request for referrals returned
- [ ] Letter/gift of your thank you sent to client
- [ ] Letter/gift of your thank you sent to introducer
- [ ] Letter of your thank you sent to helpers
- [ ] Read and code evaluations for info requests
- [ ] Calls to attendees requesting info
- [ ] Mail outs to attendees requesting info
- [ ] Extraction of best testimonials
- [ ] Best testimonials into one sheet, etc.
- [ ] BC notes re performance improvement
- [ ] BC reviews audio and video tape
- [ ] Attendees names onto mailing list
- [ ] Follow-up program with attendees
- [ ] Time-limited sale offer to attendees mailed
- [ ] File 2 sets of attendee handouts
- [ ] Toss rest of attendee handouts
- [ ] File unused speaker rating forms, bios, articles
- [ ] Re-pack all items and ready them for next program

❝   ❞

Thoughts About Speaking

A good teacher, like a good entertainer first must hold his audience's attention, then he can teach his lesson.

John Henrik Clarke

You cannot teach a man anything. You can only help him discover it within himself.

Galileo Galilei

I never teach my pupils; I only attempt to provide the conditions in which they can learn.

Albert Einstein

Speaking Program
One-Sheet Example

Are You Reaching Your Platform Potential?
Improve Your Speaking Effectiveness
In This Unique Program-

The Mental Game Of Speaking ™
Building Composure, Confidence and Credibility

Platform professionals consistently perform to their true potential. They connect with their audiences. They overcome stage fright, get into the zone and influence people in masterful ways. They know how to meet the needs of every audience they encounter. You can do all this and more when you learn the mastery secrets of professional speakers. This program will positively impact your platform confidence and speaking effectiveness.

The Mental Game Of Speaking™ helps you dramatically increase your awareness as a speaker, develop a self-coaching system and gives you a master performance blueprint for realizing your great platform potential. This is a content-rich, practical and experimential program where you will learn how to craft magical stories, use humor, inject a spirit of Hollywood into your staging and come across as the strong professional you are.

Bill was a member of the Board Of Directors of The National Speakers Association in Northern California for two years. He has trained professional speakers and corporate executives in the methods and approaches that world-class presenters utilize. He will teach you how to build a tool kit of communication and influencing skills that you will begin using immediately and will have for a lifetime. Here are some of the powerful benefits you'll receive from this experiential, entertaining and practical program. You will:

- Know how to construct a head message and heart message your audiences will love.
- Learn to read your audience so you can think on your feet and adjust your material to their needs.
- Discover how to handle disruptions and distractions and stay focused.
- Develop interactive audience-involvement approaches to keep everyone engaged.
- Look forward to holding Q and A sessions and being spontaneous.

In this program you will learn inside professional secrets of how to calibrate your audience, use facilitation techniques, pre-program questionnaires, and to craft powerful openers and closers that will make your presentations memorable. You'll learn how to create, write and stage your speeches. You'll learn how to project your body language, voice control and how to pace your speeches.

Available as a breakfast, luncheon or dinner keynote speech, or as a half-day or full day interactive workshop, **The Mental Game Of Speaking**™ can be fully customized for your group's needs. Organizations can use this program in retreats, meetings, team sessions and more.

Your platform coach is Bill Cole, MS, MA, The Mental Game Coach™ - Bill is a nationally and internationally-recognized coach and expert in peak performance. He has been a professional coach for over 30 years, including corporate America, big-time college athletics and major-league pro sports. He's a published book author with over 300 published articles worldwide to his credit.

Ask about these other winning programs: The Mental Game of Customer Service, Winning the Mental Game of Team Building, Winning the Mental Game of Golf, Winning the Mental Game of Life, The Mental Game of

Selling, Influencing Skills For Leaders, Stop Stress And Banish Burnout For Sustainable Self-Renewal and Coaching For Communication Excellence.

To book this program, or for more information, please contact us today.

WILLIAM B. COLE CONSULTANTS - Peak Performance Solutions Coaching, Consulting, Facilitating, Workshops, Seminars, Speaking, Development, Learning Tools 19925 Stevens Creek Blvd., Suite 100, Cupertino, CA 95014-2358 Voice: 408-725-7191 TOLL FREE: 888-445-0291 Fax: 408-298-9525 E-mail: Bill@MentalGameCoach.com Web Site: www.MentalGameCoach.com

From this source:
www.mentalgamecoach.com/Programs/MentalGameOfSpeaking.html

❝   ❞

Thoughts About Speaking

A good teacher must be able to put himself
in the place of those who find learning hard.

Eliphas Levi

The art of teaching is the art of assisting discovery.

Mark van Doren

Having been an educator for so many years I know that
all a good teacher can do is set a context, raise
questions or enter into a kind of a dialogic
relationship with their students.

Godfrey Reggio

Speaker Evaluation Feedback Form For The Audience

Name of speaker _____

Date of presentation _____

Location _____

Topic _____

Directions: Choose a rating number that best represents your answer to each question, and write it in the space provided.

    1. Excellent
    2. Very Good
    3. Good
    4. Fair
    5. Poor

Feel free to write in any additional comments on any question anywhere you want on this form, including the back.

1. How would you rate the presentation skills of the speaker?

   _____

2. The speaker's opening was attention-getting, and made you curious about what was to come.

   _____

3. The speaker showed an understanding of rapport, and skill in creating it and maintaining it.

   _____

4. The speaker's physical appearance was appropriate for the occasion and the audience.

   _____

5. The speaker's points were made clearly and without unnecessary detail.

_____

6. The speaker's points were presented in a logical easy-to-follow sequence.

_____

7. The terminology used and the degree of technical detail was suitable to this audience.

_____

8. The material was relevant to the purpose of the presentation.

_____

9. The speaker stayed on topic and avoided wandering and rambling.

_____

10. The material presented indicated the speaker's credibility, knowledge and understanding of the subject was:

_____

11. The speaker looked at the audience effectively and maintained good eye contact with them.

_____

12. The speaker was pleasing to listen to in terms of vocal volume and speed of delivery.

_____

13. The speaker had enough vocal variety and intonation changes to maintain interest, avoid monotony, and give emphasis where required.

_____

14. The speaker's transitions were smooth and easy to follow.

_____

15. The speaker limited filler words and distracting physical mannerisms.

    _____

16. The speaker listened well, encouraged questions and answered the questions well, giving concise and informative replies.

    _____

17. Regarding the visual aids, how was the frequency of use?

    _____

18. The slides, whiteboard writing, props, video and computer graphics contained information of real assistance in communicating the speaker's story.

    _____

19. The amount of information on slides, overheads or handouts was:

    _____

20. The visual aids were easily readable and understandable.

    _____

21. How persuasive was the speaker?

    _____

22. How was the speaker's closing?

    _____

What are the speaker's three biggest strengths?

1.

2.

3.

What are the speaker's three biggest weaknesses?

1.

2.

3.

What other advice would you have for the speaker in terms of their delivery, content or anything else?

❝ ❞
Thoughts About Speaking

The only kind of learning which significantly influences behavior is self-discovered or self-appropriated learning - truth that has been assimilated in experience.

Carl Rogers

The teacher if he is indeed wise does not teach bid you to enter the house of wisdom but leads you to the threshold of your own mind.

Kahlil Gilbran

The real voyage of discovery consists not in seeking new lands, but in seeing with new eyes.

Marcel Proust

Post-Presentation Analysis Chart

Bill Cole, MS, MA.

Name _____

Date and Time of Speech _____

Type of Speech _____

Location of Speech _____

Rate your performance in this presentation from 1-5, with 5 excellent, 4 very good, 3 average, 2 fair and 1 poor. This presentation: _____. Now write your answers to these questions.

1. What did you really LIKE about your performance in this presentation?

2. What do you wish you WOULD have done this time?

3. What do you wish you HAD NOT done this time?

4. How was YOUR INTRODUCTION by another person?

5. How was your START to your presentation?

6. How was your CLOSE to your presentation?

7. How was the QUESTION-ANSWER period in your presentation?

8. What was your GAME PLAN (What were you attempting to accomplish, and how?) going into this presentation?

9. What strategies did you ACTUALLY USE in this presentation?

10. What strategies worked WELL?

11. What strategies did NOT work well?

12. How was your audience CONNECTION AND RAPPORT?

13. Were there any heckler or audience DISRUPTION/RESISTANCE SITUATIONS and if so, how did you handle them?

14. What FEEDBACK (direct and indirect, verbal and non-verbal) did people give you?

15. What IMPACT do you believe your presentation had on the audience?

16. What would you do DIFFERENTLY next time?

17. Overall, how was your MENTAL GAME (nerves, getting into the zone, etc)?

18. How well did the TECHNICAL ASPECTS (lighting, sound, visual) of your program work out?

19. How well did the AUDIENCE HANDOUTS (workbook, manual, etc.) in your program work out?

20. How well did you control the overall ROOM DYNAMICS (staging, assistants, room configuration, etc), before, during and after the program?

21. In a nutshell, why did you SUCCEED, or why did you NOT SUCCEED?

22. If you had this presentation TO DO OVER AGAIN, what would you do DIFFERENTLY?

23. What did you LEARN from this presentation?

24. What will you do DIFFERENTLY IN YOUR PRACTICES and training to benefit from the wisdom you gained from this presentation?

❝ ❞

Thoughts About Speaking

The mediocre teacher tells. The good teacher explains.
The superior teacher demonstrates.
The great teacher inspires.

William Arthur Ward

I cannot teach anybody anything.
I can only make them think.

Socrates

What I hear, I forget. What I see, I remember.
What I do, I understand.

Confucius

Speaking Program Equipment Request

To make Bill Cole's program as successful as possible, the following equipment will be needed. If there is any question or difficulty in securing the equipment, please call and discuss it with us well before the program. Excellent programs are based on taking care of all the little details ahead of time. We do everything we can from our end to do make everything run smoothly. We appreciate everything you can do from your end!

Audio Equipment Needed:

_____ Lavalier microphone

_____ 25 foot microphone cord

_____ Cordless lavalier microphone

_____ We will supply our own cordless microphone

Visual Equipment Needed:

_____ Slide projector with remote slide changer

_____ VCR and large screen monitor

_____ Large projector screen

_____ Overhead projector

_____ Free-standing easel with paper pad attached

Other Equipment Needed:

_____ Bar stool

_____ Music stand

_____ Lectern

_____ Six foot draped table at front of room

_____ Six foot draped table at front of room

❝   ❞

Thoughts About Speaking

Learning is not a spectator sport.

D. Blocher

When I give up trying to impress the group, I become very impressive. Let go in order to achieve. The wise facilitator speaks rarely and briefly, teaching more through being than doing.

The Tao Te Ching

There are two ways of being creative. One can sing and dance. Or one can create an environment in which singers and dancers flourish.

Warren Bennis

Wanted

Your Success Stories And Best Tips
To Help Others Succeed In Speaking

Want to share your great ideas about public speaking with others? Send me your top speaking tips, techniques, stories, quotes and how-to-tactics that helped you succeed and you can then make a positive impact on others who have an important message to share with the world.

I love feedback. I would really enjoy hearing how you have put the ideas in this book into action and how they have helped you succeed.

I also want to hear from you about issues and challenges I did not include in this first edition. In what areas do you need more help? What do you need to know further to succeed faster?

Reward

In addition to the good feeling you'll get in helping others, I want to give you recognition. If I accept your story or success tip I will publish it in my next book. You will receive credit for the submission, along with a listing of your contact information.

When you send me your tip, be sure to include your name, organization, title, phone number, street address, web site and e-mail address. I prefer to receive your submissions via email for easier handling.

I really want to hear from you!

About Bill Cole

Bill Cole, MS, MA is a nationally-known presentation skills coaching and training expert. He is a speech writer and presentation coach to professional speakers and trainers, executives, business professionals, educators, politicians and everyday folks who just want to give a good speech and not break out in a sweat.

www.mentalgamecoach.com

"Bill Cole is a world-class coach... A speaker's speaker."

National Speakers Association

"a veteran professional communicator"

Linear Technology Corporation

Bill received extensive training in standup comedy, improv, joke writing and speech humor writing from some of the top professionals in the comedy world. Bill is also a graduate of the San Francisco Comedy College, the largest stand-up comedy school in the country.

Bill has trained professional speakers on public speaking skills in his proprietary and popular workshop **The Mental Game of Speaking™ Building Composure, Confidence and Credibility:**

www.mentalgamecoach.com/Programs/MentalGameOfS peaking.html

Bill is also one of the most prominent, prolific and successful performance psychology consultants working today. He has been the mental game coach or sports psychology consultant with athletes or coaches of 19 world and national teams, nine international and Olympic teams, 32 professional sports teams, associations or leagues, and of athletes who have won 36 world and national championships. He has been the mental trainer for thousands of athletes in over 100 sports, at all ages and skill levels.

"Bill Cole is a leading Olympic sports psychologist and a world-renowned peak performance coach."

British Broadcasting Corporation (The BBC)

"Bill Cole is a leading author on sports psychology."

Yahoo! Sports

Bill Cole is also the author of ten publications:

Books:

- The Interview Success Guide

- Test Stress Success Manual

- Championship Tennis

- The Mental Game of Golf

- Mental Game of Sports Mental Training Manual

- The Cole Mental Game of Sports Assessment Tool (CMGSAT)

Audiobooks:

- Winning the Mental Game of Life

- Stop Stress And Banish Burnout For Sustainable Self-Renewal

- The Mental Game of Motorcycle Racing

- The Psychology of Golf: Manage Mental Errors

Bill holds a BS in Sport Psychology from SUNY-Buffalo, an MS in Physical Education from CSU-Fullerton and an MA in Counseling Psychology from Santa Clara University.

Thoughts About Speaking

When you know something, say what you know. When you don't know something, say that you don't know. That is knowledge.

Confucius

The art of teaching is the art of assisting discovery.

Mark Van Doren

There can be no knowledge without emotion. We may be aware of a truth, yet until we have felt its force, it is not ours. To the cognition of the brain must be added the experience of the soul.

Arnold Bennett

Glossary Of Terms
In Public Speaking

This glossary contains 218 words and phrases used in public speaking.

Ad Lib: Spontaneous or seemingly spontaneous words spoken during a presentation.

Agent: An individual who contracts to represent a speaker or celebrity for a commission.

Amphitheater-Style Seating: Tiered seating like that found in a movie theater.

ASTD: The Association for Training and Development, a professional association for trainers, management consultants and human resources professionals.

Associations: Professional organizations where people with similar interests join to gain educational, professional, financial and social advantages.

Attendees: Anyone who is present at a meeting, convention, program or session where speeches are made.

Audience: Attendees at a program who hear a speaker. (See attendees)

Audience Participation: Having the audience respond or participate, rather than just listen.

Autograph table: A table in the back of the room where a speaker signs books, autographs and other products following a presentation.

A/V: Abbreviation for audio-visual equipment including any multi-media, sound, projection or equipment used in a presentation.

Back Of Room Sales: Product sales that take place at a presentation, often called BOR.

Banquet Style Seating: Where the audience is seated at round tables, usually eight to ten to a table. Very awkward for the person whose back is to the speaker.

Bid: An offer in fee level or payment negotiation a client makes for speaker services.

Bio: A speaker's biography and background, germane to topic and market niche.

Bio Sheet: A one-page speaker's biography and background, germane to topic and market niche.

Blocking: The positioning of you and your equipment on the stage and in the presentation room in relationship to the audience.

Booking: Making an engagement date to speak on a speaker's calendar.

Break-Out: Splitting a larger audience group into smaller units to conduct separate sessions. Sometimes called break-out session.

Breakout Speaker: A speaker who gives 90-minutes to 3-hours of focused content and usually covers one topic in depth and gives the audience an outline to follow.

Bridges: Transitions or connecting points in a speech, from thought to thought. See transition.

Brochure: A promotional flyer or multi-fold piece that contains a speaker's best marketing approaches, such as testimonials, client lists, speech titles and descriptions, bio and contact information.

Bulk Mail: Mail that goes out en mass to reduce postal rates.

Bureau: An agency or booking business that hires speakers for their clients. They are usually paid a percentage of the speaking fee.

Business Card: A small card a speaker gives out to promote his business.

Business Plan: A strategic and tactical formulation that guides a speaker's business in numerous areas, from financial to marketing to operations.

Cancellation clause: The clause in a speaker's contract that specifies the penalties if a program is canceled.

Cancellations: The act of the client calling off a presentation.

Case Study: A detailed, real-world, or contrived example used to highlight and make clear a speaker's concept.

Cavett Award: The highest award in the National Speakers Association, for the speaker of the year.

CEU's: Continuing Educational Units.

Circle Seating Style: Where the audience is seated in a circle around a speaker or presenter.

Classroom Seating Style: Where the audience is seated in parallel rows behind tables facing the speaker.

Client: The entity that pays the speaker, which may be a corporation, association, educational institution, non-profit, or governmental agency.

Closing: The final section of a speech the speaker uses to make a final point or to bring the audience to action.

Cold Calling: Telephone sales calls made to suspects, or to people who do not know the speaker.

Concurrent Session: A break-out session that runs at the same time as other sessions.

Conference-Style Seating: Where the audience is seated in parallel rows without tables facing the speaker.

Consultant: An expert who analyzes a specific business problem and prescribes a solution. He or she may be involved in the carrying out of the solution and may be paid by the hour, day or week or flat project fee.

Consulting: The work a speaker does that does not include speaking or training, such as writing, coaching, assessment, facilitating and advice.

Content: Material in a presentation that is useful beyond mere entertainment value.

Contract: The legal document between the speaker and the agent, bureau, manager or client, containing what each will do and considerations for each.

Convention: A large gathering of people with similar interests where a speaker would present.

Copyrights: Statements and symbols signifying the legal ownership of articles, books, tapes and other products or business names or processes that a speaker produces.

Cordless Microphone: A microphone that uses a transmitter instead of a cord to send the signal to receiver, then to an amplifier, and then to the sound speakers. May be prone to interference from other devices using the same frequency.

Corporate Training: Training that is done for a corporate client, usually on their premises.

Cover Letter: The letter that goes out with a promotional package or press kit, explaining the reason for the mailing.

CPAE: The Council of Peers Award of Excellence: The Hall of Fame for speakers in the National Speakers Association.

Cruise Ship Speaking: Speaking on board ships, sometimes for pay and sometimes for trade of room and board.

CSP: Certified Speaking Professional, the highest earned designation from the National Speakers Association.

Customization: The degree to which a speaker modifies a speech or product material to fit the needs of the client and audience.

Dais: A raised platform the speaker stands on. Also called a podium, riser or stage.

Delivery: What a speaker does during a performance. This is the speaker's style, flair, drama and persona in action.

Demo: An audiotape or videotape used to promote yourself to meeting planners and other potential clients.

Direct Mail: Mail sent to a particular person, rather than to a business or occupant.

Downstage: The part of the stage closest to the audience.

Dynamic Range: The variances in voice, volume, gestures, tone, etc., a speaker may use in a performance.

Easel: A stand used to support visual aids such as flip charts or graphics.

Elevator Speech: A brief (usually 30 seconds or less) advertisement you provide to someone the first time you meet them, describing your services and business.

Emcee: An informal term for the master of ceremonies, or announcer or introducer at a program. Also known as MC.

Emerging Speaker: A speaker new to the speaking profession.

Endorsement: A quote, phrase or letter of testimonial from someone who has seen you speak, attesting to your abilities.

Engagement: A speaking date you have booked. Also called a gig.

Expenses: Any business-related out of pocket expenses incurred while you travel to or from a speaking date.

Extemporaneous: Any spur of the moment, impromptu or spontaneous presentation.

Facilitation: The process of guiding a group through awareness and educational exercises. Some speaking is involved.

Fee: Payment for speaking, consulting, facilitating or other services.

Fee Levels: The various fee segments in the business, ranging from novice, emerging, journeyman, established to celebrity.

Firm Date: A speaking engagement that is confirmed and guaranteed by the client.

Flipchart: The paper you write on that goes on an easel.

Flyer: A circular or piece of marketing collateral you send out to obtain bookings.

Focus: Specific intent of a talk or speech.

Freebies: Trade or gratis speeches you give in return for some or all of the following exposure: practice, testimonials, referrals, bartered goods or services.

General Assembly: The time, other than meal time, when all attendees of a meeting convene.

General Session: The time when all attendees of a meeting convene to hear a keynote.

Gig: A speaking date or engagement.

Give-Aways: Free items the speaker gives to the audience that helps them continue their learning at home and that promotes the speaker.

Glossy: Biography or one-sheet printing on heavy, shiny paper.

Handout: Any paper, report, handbook, workbook or item the speaker gives the audience.

Handheld Microphone: A microphone you use from your hand.

Hands Free Mike: A microphone you wear that either attaches to your lapel or hangs around your neck. Sometimes called a "lavaliere" or "lapel mic".

Head Table: The table where dignitaries, leaders, directors or important guests sit at a luncheon or dinner program.

Heart Story: A story that touches the heart instead of the head.

Heckler: Someone who attempts to interrupt your presentation, either by talking or by making noise.

Honorarium: Small stipend for speaking or related services.

House Lights: Lighting that shines on the audience rather than the speaker.

Humorist: A speaker who uses funny material to entertain and enhance speech content.

Ice-Breakers: Exercises designed to loosen up an audience, to prepare them to receive a speaker and each other.

IGAB: The International Group of Agents and Bureaus, a professional association for businesses that book speakers.

In-Bound Marketing: Turning telephone inquiries into bookings through effective persuasion and sales techniques.

In-House: A presentation made on the client's site.

Introducer: The person who presents a speaker to the audience via a brief speaker bio and lead-in of the speaker's reasons for being there.

Interactive Training: Hands-on or experiential exercises designed to get the audience involved fully, rather than just in a listening mode.

Introduction: A brief biography and reason the speaker is giving the speech, spoken by an introducer.

Impromptu Speech: An extemporaneous speech, devised on the spot.

Island Seating Style: Where audience members sit in groups or "islands".

Keynote: The main speech given to most, if not all, the attendees in one general session.

Keynote Speaker: A speaker who kicks off a conference, usually with 60-90 minutes of motivational and high-energy speaking, using lots of stories and humor with a minimum of content.

Keynoter: The person giving the keynote.

Kill Fee: Payment made to the speaker should the client cancel the program without sufficient notice.

Lavalier: A microphone, with or without a cord, that is either worn around the neck, or attached to clothing. Considered to be a hands-free microphone.

Lectern: A stand for holding the speaker's notes and other speaking equipment and props.

Letter Of Agreement: A legal document between speaker and client, less formal than a contract.

Licensing: The selling of temporary use permits to an organization for a speaker's materials or products.

Master Of Ceremonies: A person who hosts parties and events in an enjoyable manner by keeping events on time, announcing people and program events and setting the proper tone. See MC.

MC: Master of ceremonies.

Mailing House: A business that handles outgoing and/or incoming mail. This may include product orders and fulfillment, mailing lists, newsletters and other products of the speaker.

Mailing List: A list of names a speaker uses to mail marketing material.

Manager: A person who handles a speaker's business details.

Marketing: Efforts directed to promoting, advertising and making a speaker known to a particular niche.

Media Kit: A speaker's press kit sent to potential clients and the media, to promote the speaking business. It may contain a bio, articles, one-sheets, program descriptions, client lists and testimonials. See press kit.

Meeting Planner: The coordinator or organizer in charge of logistics for the entire meeting or convention.

Mentor: An experienced speaker who coaches a less-experienced speaker.

Menu Of Services: The range of services a speaker offers to clients.

Mic: A written abbreviation for the word microphone, pronounced "mike".

Mike: An abbreviation for the word microphone.

Moderator: The person in a panel, debate, roundtable or meeting who controls and organizes its conduct.

Motivational Speaker: A speaker who attempts to inspire, i.e., make the audience behave differently and be entertaining at the same time.

MPI: Acronym for Meeting Planners International.

Multiday: A program presented over more than one day.

Multimedia: The use of varied media to enhance a presentation. This may include slides, computer-generated images, overheads, music, film, video and more.

NSA: Acronym for National Speakers Association.

Newsletter: A regularly mailed hard-copy or electronic report designed to educate clients and promote a speaker's business.

Off The Shelf: A turnkey, standard or boiler-plate speech or program, one that is not customized to the client's needs.

One Sheet: The piece of marketing collateral that announces a speaker's programs, bio, client list, contact information and other branding or marketing information. May be one-sided or two-sided.

On-Site Training: Training provided at the client's place of business.

Opening: The very start of a speech, as the speaker begins after being introduced.

Open Enrollment Program: A speaking, training or workshop program for which the public may enroll.

Outbound Marketing: Communications sent to potential clients via telephone, direct mail, fax, e-mail or other media intended to induce them to book a speaker.

Outline: The brief sketch or speech overview used by a speaker, and possibly used as handout for the audience.

Overhead Projector: An illumination device that shows transparencies on a screen.

PA System: The public address sound system used in a program.

PR (Public Relations): Promotions, advertising, publicity and other strategies used to make the speaker more visibility in a chosen market.

Panel: A group of speakers or experts who discuss a topic, often with question and answer format from the audience.

Partial Exclusive: An exclusive agreement with a speaker in a restricted market segment, either via area or by market niche.

Per Diem: Payment for daily expenses a speaker incurs, or for consulting services per day.

Platform: A dais, riser, podium or stage that the speaker stands on.

Plenary: The general or main session or gathering at a meeting or convention.

Plug: Making a pitch on the platform for a speaker's book, tapes or other products and services.

Podium: A dais, riser, platform or stage that the speaker stands on.

Positioning: How a speaker and or his products and services are specially differentiated in the marketplace.

Power Pack: A group of products sold as a single unit, as a special or sale price, usually at an engagement.

Power Point: A software program from Microsoft® used for making multi-media presentations.

PPQ (Pre-Program Questionnaire): The multiple page assessment tool sent to the client to determine how the program will be customized.

Premiums: Promotional items given to clients or audience members usually containing a speaker's contact information.

Press Kit: The package of information, usually in a folder, used to promote a speaker. It may contain a bio, articles one-sheets, program descriptions client lists and testimonials. See media kit.

Press Release: A promotional notice sent out announcing a news-worthy accomplishment or item by a speaker.

Presentation Software: A computer application used to create and develop multimedia images and sound supporting a speech.

Pricing: The fee and product and services price points a speaker sets.

Professional Speaker: A speaker who is paid a fee or honorarium for a performance.

Product: The books, reports, audios, videos, CD's, workbooks, diskettes, posters, etc. that a speaker sells to the client or to the audience.

Projector: Equipment for illuminating a picture. May be a slide, overhead, computer or movie projector.

Promotion: Usually a discount for a limited time designed to induce meeting planners to try a speaker.

Promotions: Anything designed to increase awareness on the part of meeting planners about a speaker. Could be advertising, public relations or other materials.

Prompter: An electronic display device that projects the speaker's notes onto a screen so they may be read by the speaker, but by no one else. See teleprompter.

Proposal: A suggested outline of services and products a speaker provides to a client for review, for potential purchase.

Prop: Abbreviation for property, any item used by the speaker to enhance his or her performance, including magic items or conversation pieces.

Proprietary: A speaker's original material, products, names or processes owned by the speaker.

Prospects: Potential customers or clients who might hire a speaker.

Public Address System: The sound system used in a program. Also called a PA system

Publicity: Any marketing or promotional activity a speaker does to advance his or her name recognition and visibility in the marketplace.

Public Domain: Material, music, names, titles or other content that is not owned by any individual or business. Anyone may use them.

Public Seminar: Any program available to the public.

Public Speaker: An individual who speaks in public, paid or not.

Q and A: The period of a presentation when the speaker takes questions from the audience. Called question and answer.

Rapport: The intimate, trusting relationship forged between the speaker and the audience.

Rave: A testimonial quote or letter from a satisfied client or meeting planner. See testimonial.

Referral: The name of another business or organization that the speaker may contact for potential future business.

Rehearsal: Practicing or reviewing the presentation, either actually or mentally.

Retreat: A place and time when a group goes away from their normal work setting to reflect, renew and accomplish certain tasks.

Role Playing: A simulation where people take on personas in a dramatic-like manner to make a point about some aspect of business or life.

Room Set-Up: The manner in which the audience seating is set up for a presentation. See seating arrangements.

Sales Cycle: The period of time and various processes the sales pipeline goes through, from initial contact to close of the sale.

Script: A written procedure for conducting a sales call. Also a speaker's written notes.

Seating Arrangements: The manner in which the audience seating is set up for a presentation. See room set-up.

Self-Publishing: The writing, printing, marketing and distribution of a book, audio, video, CD or other product by the speaker alone. Costs are borne by the speaker.

Selling From The Platform: The art of convincing the audience that they need the products and services the speaker makes available during and after the program.

Seminar: A presentation that may be 30 minutes to multiple days in duration.

Seminar Companies: Companies that hire speakers to travel and conduct public programs on various topics.

Seminar Leader: A speaker who gives 3-hours to 6-hours or even several days of very in-depth coverage on one or several topics. Usually provides the audience with a workbook.

Showcase: A free, or usually free, speech a speaker gives to provide exposure to potential clients.

Simulations: A reality-like game or situation where people take on personas in a dramatic-like manner to make a point about some aspect of business or life.

Signature Story: A speaker's original and easily-recognized personal story.

Site-License Fees: Payment a speaker charges a company to use products in their company only, such as manuals, books, tapes, workbooks and assessments.

Slides: Either an overhead transparency or a 35 mm, small transparency going into a slide projector.

Sound Bites: Short, pithy quotes or phrases used to help a speaker be memorable.

Sound Man: The person handling the AV and usually all other multi-media in a presentation.

Sound System: Music or vocal projection equipment used in a program. Also called a PA System

Speaker Rating Sheet: A one-page form evaluating the speaker, filled out by the audience.

Smile Sheet: Same as speaker rating sheet, but may have less detail.

Speech: The actual program a speaker presents to the audience.

Staff: Anyone who assists the speaker, either in the office or on-site.

Stage: Where the speaker stands to deliver the program.

Stage Left: The side of the stage to the performer's left as he faces the audience.

Stage Right: The side of the stage to the performer's right as he faces the audience.

Stage Directions: Physical location points for the speaker to use once on stage during a performance.

Stage Fright: Anxiety or nervousness around a performance.

Suspects: Potential purchasers of a speaker's services or products, who do not know the speaker yet.

Tailoring Material: Customizing presentation material to the client and audience.

Team Building: Developing new or established teams for better trust, cohesion and functioning.

Teleprompter: An electronic display device that projects the speaker's notes onto a screen so they may be read by the speaker, but by no one else. See prompter.

Tentative Date: A hold on a date by the speaker for a client, even though there is no firm commitment from the buyer.

Testimonial: A congratulatory or praising quote or letter from a satisfied client or meeting planner. See rave.

Theater Seating Style: See amphitheater style seating.

Toastmasters International: A world-wide organization of people who focus on the learning and promotion of the art of speaking.

Trade Out: The bartering of speaking services for goods or services, rather than cash-only payment.

Trainer: A person who presents training or workshops or seminars.

Transparency: A clear plastic sheet viewed by light shining through it. Can be written on or materials may be printed on it.

Transitions: Bridges or connecting points in a speech, from thought to thought. See bridge.

Upstage: Position on the stage farthest from the audience. May also refer to one speaker stealing the audience's attention from another.

Ups-Unique-Selling Proposition: That which makes one program or speaker different from another.

U-Shaped Seating Style: Where the audience is seated in a horseshoe arrangement with the speaker positioned at the opening of the "U".

Venue: The place where a meeting, convention or speech takes place.

Visual Aids: Any physical props or projections a speaker uses to enhance the content for the audience.

Web Site: A visual, and sometimes audio, package a speaker creates for people to visit on the World Wide Web.

Wings: The sides of the stage, out of sight of the audience.

Workshop: A hands-on experiential program lasting from one hour to multiple days.

Workbook: An educational handout, usually multiple pages, a speaker creates for the audience to enhance their understanding of the speech content, and as added take-away value.

Index

399

www.ingramcontent.com/pod-product-compliance
Lightning Source LLC
Chambersburg PA
CBHW060236100426
42742CB00011B/1551

* 9 7 8 1 9 3 1 8 2 5 1 6 0 *